Water Works

a physical science unit for high-ability learners in grades k–1

Water Works

Project Clarion Primary Science Units
Funded by the Jacob K. Javits Program, United Stated Department of Education

The College of William and Mary
School of Education
Center for Gifted Education
P.O. Box 8795
Williamsburg, VA 23187-8795

Co-Principal Investigators: Bruce A. Bracken, Ph.D., and Joyce VanTassel-Baska, Ed.D.
Project Managers: Tamra Stambaugh, Ph.D., Janice Robbins, Ph.D., and Valerie Gregory, Ed.D.
Unit Developers: Peggy Jaquot, Janice Robbins, Ph.D., and Elizabeth B. Sutton

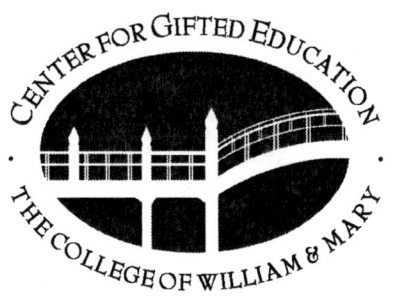

Copyright ©2008 Center for Gifted Education, The College of William and Mary

Edited by Lacy Elwood
Production Design by Marjorie Parker

ISBN-13: 978-1-59363-327-1
ISBN-10: 1-59363-327-0

The purchase of this book entitles the buyer to reproduce student activity pages for classroom use only. Other use requires written permission of publisher. All rights reserved.

At the time of this book's publication, all facts and figures cited are the most current available; all telephone numbers, addresses, and Web site URLs are accurate and active; all publications, organizations, Web sites, and other resources exist as described in this book; and all have been verified. The authors and Prufrock Press make no warranty or guarantee concerning the information and materials given out by organizations or content found at Web sites, and we are not responsible for any changes that occur after this book's publication. If you find an error or believe that a resource listed here is not as described, please contact Prufrock Press.

Prufrock Press Inc.
P.O. Box 8813
Waco, TX 76714-8813
Phone: (800) 998-2208
Fax: (800) 240-0333
http://www.prufrock.com

Contents

Part One: Unit Overview
Introduction to the Unit 2
Unit Glossary 8
Teacher's Guide to Content 9
Teaching Resources 11

Part Two: Lesson Plans
Lesson Overview 13
Lesson 1: What Is a Scientist? 16
Lesson 2: What Is Change? 23
Lesson 3: What Scientists Do: Observe, Ask Questions, Learn More 28
Lesson 4: What Scientists Do: Experiment, Create Meaning, Tell Others 32
Lesson 5: What Are Sources of Water on Earth? 38
Lesson 6: Does Water Disappear? 40
Lesson 7: Can Water Reappear? 46
Lesson 8: What Happens When Water Is Mixed With Other Liquids? 49
Lesson 9: What Is Density? 54
Lesson 10: Which Things Sink and Float? 58
Lesson 11: Can We Make a Better Floater? 62
Lesson 12: What Have We Learned About Water? 68

Appendices
Appendix A: Science Safety 74
Appendix B: Teaching Models 78
Appendix C: Basic Concepts 89
Appendix D: Assessment Package 90
References 129

Part One: Unit Overview

Introduction to the Unit

The unit *Water Works* engages kindergarten and first-grade students in close observations and experimentation about water. The overarching concept of change is reinforced as students notice, react to, reflect on, and discover more about force and change. Students ask questions and design experiments to reinforce their learning. Generalizations about how things change are developed through students' analysis of their findings. Students explore the characteristics of water, discover which objects sink and which objects float, experiment to make things float, and examine materials and their interactions with water.

The Project Clarion Science Units for Primary Grades have been designed to introduce young students to science concepts, science processes, and overarching concepts. A hands-on, constructivist approach is used to allow children to build their knowledge base and their skills as they explore science topics through play and planned investigations (see Appendix A for science safety skills to introduce to your students as they undertake each Project Clarion Science Unit). Students are engaged in creative and critical thinking, problem finding and solving, process skill development, and communication opportunities. Each unit is designed to strengthen essential concepts including quantity, direction/position, comparison, colors, letter identification, numbers/counting, size, self-/social awareness, texture/material, shape, and time/sequence. The units also focus on overarching concepts of systems, patterns, change, and cause and effect.

Essential Understandings of the Unit

Through completion of this unit, the student will convey the following essential understandings:
- Our senses help us to seek, find, and react to information.
- Water can take different forms (solid, liquid, gas) but it is still water.
- The state of water can change by heating or cooling.
- The natural flow of water is downhill.
- Water evaporates into the air.
- Water condenses on cold surfaces.
- Some liquids will separate when mixed with water. Others will not.
- Some substances will dissolve in water. Others will not.
- Certain objects float in water while others do not float.
- Density is the relationship between the volume of an object and its mass.

Concepts Covered in This Unit

Many teachers find concept mapping useful for envisioning the scope of a lesson or unit. Teachers also use student-developed concept maps as a way of measuring student progress. Each Project Clarion unit contains an overview concept map (see Figure 1) that displays the essential knowledge included in the lessons and the connections students should be able to make as a result of their experiences within the unit. This overview may be useful as a classroom poster that teachers and students can refer to throughout the unit.

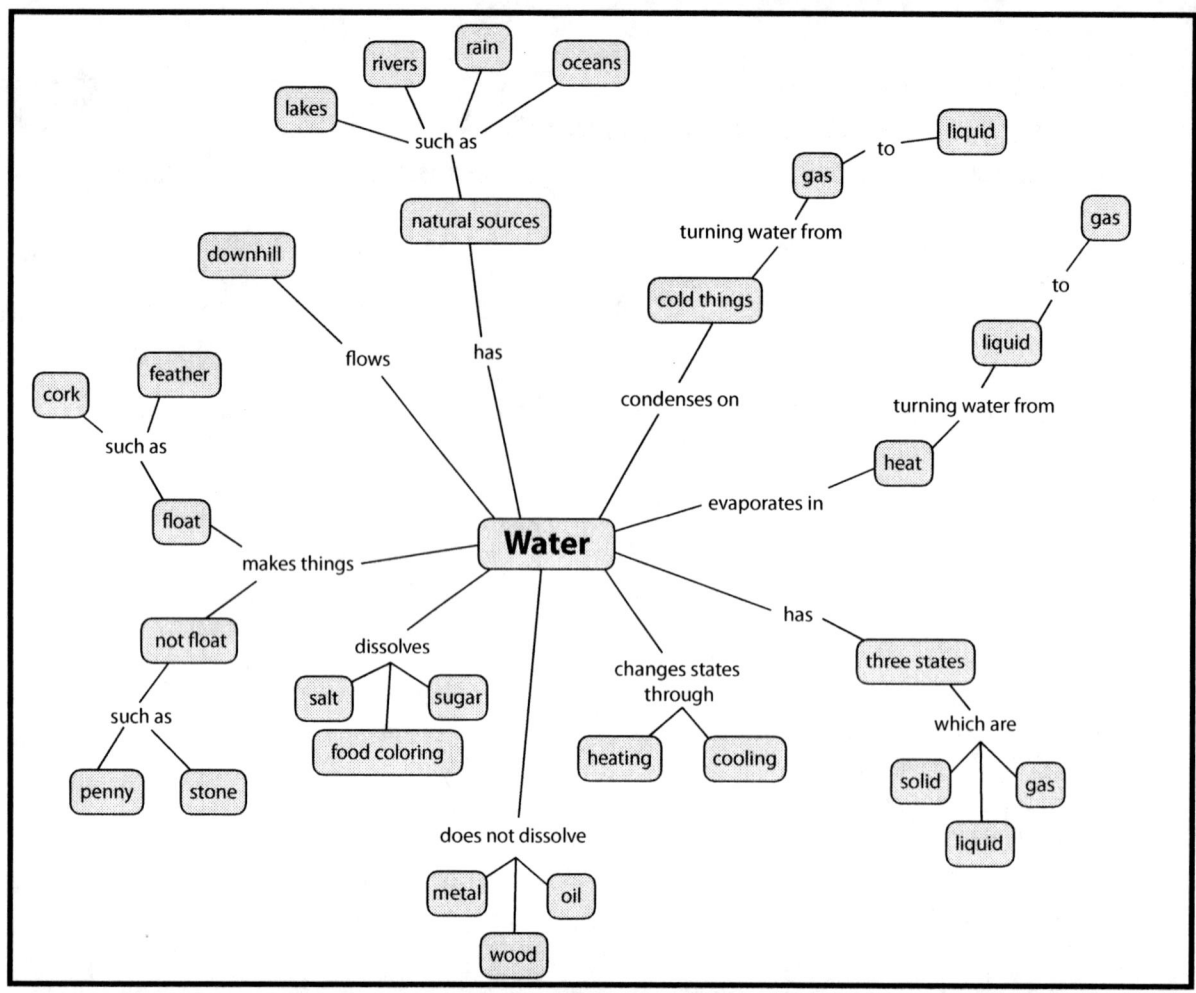

Figure 1. Water Works concept map.

Practice in using concept maps supports students' learning as they begin to build upon known concepts. Students begin to add new concepts to their initial understanding of a topic and to make new connections between concepts. The use of concept maps within the lessons also helps teachers to recognize students' conceptual frameworks so that instruction can be adapted as necessary. More information on concept maps can be found in Appendix B. Other information on assessing students' understandings of concepts is included in Appendix C.

Overarching Concept

The overarching concept for this unit is *change*. The natural world changes continually. Some changes may be too slow to observe. Students begin to understand the concept of change in science by learning about changes over time, as well as manmade changes that impact conditions.

The second lesson in this unit introduces the concept of change. This lesson is based on Hilda Taba's Concept Development Model (Taba, 1962; see Appendix B). Students are asked to brainstorm examples of change, categorize their examples, identify nonexamples of the concept, and make generalizations about the concept. The following generalizations about change are incorporated into this unit of study:

- Change is everywhere.
- Change relates to time.
- Change can be natural or manmade.
- Change may be random or predictable.

Change is integrated throughout unit lessons and deepens students' understanding of water. Students examine the relationship of important ideas, abstractions, and issues through the application of generalizations about the concept. For example, the Concluding Questions section of the lesson plans often includes a question that specifically addresses select change generalizations and requires students to make applications to essential science understandings. This higher level thinking enhances students' ability to think like a scientist (see Appendix B and the Taba Model of Concept Development). Moreover, teachers should assess students' ability to apply the concepts by seeking evidence that they:
- understand that change is everywhere,
- demonstrate the impact of time on change,
- articulate the nature of natural vs. manmade changes, and
- evaluate the nature of change in selected phenomena.

Scientific Investigation and Reasoning

Through participation in *Water Works,* students are guided through the process of scientific investigation. Simulating the work of real scientists, students develop a systematic set of inquiry skills.

The Wheel of Scientific Investigation and Reasoning (see Appendix B) is introduced as part of several lessons in the unit. These lessons help students to come to a better understanding of what scientists do. The six components of scientific investigation are:
- Make observations.
- Ask questions.
- Learn more.
- Design and conduct experiments.
- Create meaning from experiments.
- Tell others what was found from the experiment.

Students apply the components of scientific investigation throughout the unit and use the Wheel of Scientific Investigation and Reasoning to analyze aspects of an investigation, including the following understandings.
- To make observations, scientists use their senses, as well as instruments, to note details, identify similarities and differences, and record changes in phenomena.
- Observations about familiar objects or events often lead to the development of important questions that can spark further investigation.
- Investigation requires a careful review of what is known and what additional information must be sought.
- An experiment is a fair test designed to answer a question.
- Scientific investigations require careful gathering and analysis of data.
- To communicate findings, one must provide a clear description of what question was asked, what prediction was made, what experiment was conducted, what data were collected and analyzed, and what conclusions and inferences were developed.

Curriculum Framework

Table 1 provides an overview of the curriculum framework for Project Clarion Science Units, including student goals and outcomes.

Table 1
Project Clarion: Curriculum Framework

Goal	Student Outcomes The student will be able to:
1. Develop basic concepts related to understanding the world of science.	• Provide examples, illustrations, and salient features of important concepts. • Categorize and/or classify various concepts. • Identify counterexamples of specific concepts. • Create definition/generalizations about individual concepts including color, letter identification, numbers, size, comparison, shape, direction/position, self-/social awareness, texture/material, quantity, and time/sequence.
2. Develop the overarching concept of change.	• Understand that change is everywhere. • Demonstrate the impact of time on change. • Articulate the nature of natural vs. manmade changes. • Evaluate the nature of change in selected phenomena. • Demonstrate the impact of time on change.
3. Develop knowledge of selected content topics.	• Identify and describe the senses. • Identify examples of different states of water (solid, liquid, gas). • Describe natural flow of water. • Predict whether items will float or sink. • Explain in own words the concept of density.
4. Develop interrelated science process skills.	• Make observations. • Ask questions. • Learn more. • Design and conduct experiments. • Create meaning. • Tell others what was found.
5. Develop critical thinking skills.	• Describe problematic situations or issues. • Define relevant concepts. • Identify different points of view in situations or issues. • Describe evidence or data supporting a point of view in a situation or issue. • Draw conclusions based on data (making inferences). • Predict consequences.
6. Develop creative thinking.	• Develop fluency when naming objects and ideas, based on a stimulus. • Develop flexible thinking. • Elaborate on ideas presented in oral or written form. • Create products that replicate and extend conceptual understanding.
7. Develop curiosity and interest in the world of science.	• Express reactions about discrepant events. • Ask meaningful questions about science topics. • Articulate ideas of interest about science. • Demonstrate persistence in completing science tasks.

Standards Met

Table 2 displays how the *Water Works* unit aligns to the National Science Education Standards.

Table 2
Water Works Alignment to Standards

Standard	Fundamental Concepts	Unit Lesson
Content Standard A: Abilities necessary to do scientific inquiry.	• Ask a question about objects, organisms, and events in the environment. • Plan and conduct a simple investigation. • Employ simple equipment and tools to gather data and extend the senses. • Use data to construct a reasonable explanation. • Communicate investigations and explanations.	1, 2, 3, 4, 5, 6, 7, 8, 9, 10, 11, 12
Content Standard A: Understanding about scientific inquiry.	• Scientific investigations involve asking and answering a question and comparing the answer with what scientists already know about the world. • Scientists use different kinds of investigations depending on the questions they are trying to answer. Types of investigations include: describing objects, events, and organisms; classifying them; and doing a fair test (experimenting). • Simple instruments, such as magnifiers, thermometers, and rulers provide more information then scientists obtain using only their senses. • Scientists develop explanations using observations (evidence) and what they already know about the world (scientific knowledge). Good explanations are based on evidence from investigations. • Scientists make the results of their investigations public; they describe the investigations in ways that enable others to repeat the investigations. • Scientists review and ask questions about the results of other scientists' work.	1, 2, 3, 4, 5, 6, 7, 8, 9, 10, 11, 12
Content Standard B: Properties of objects and materials.	• Objects have many observable properties, including size, weight, shape, color, temperature, and the ability to react with other substances. Those properties can be measured using tools such as rulers, balances, and thermometers. • Materials can exists in different states: solids, liquids, and gases. Some common materials, such as water, can be changed from one state to another by heating or cooling.	3, 5, 6, 7, 8, 9, 10, 11, 12
Content Standard B: Position and motion of objects.	• The position of an object can be described by locating it relative to another object or the background.	5, 8, 10
Content Standard E: Abilities of technological design.	• Identify a simple problem. • Propose a solution. • Implement proposed solution. • Evaluate a product or design. • Communicate a problem, design, and solution.	4, 11, 12
Content Standard E: Understanding about science and technology.	• People have always had questions about their world. Science is one way of answering questions and explaining the natural world. • Women and men of all ages, backgrounds, and groups engage in a variety of scientific and technological work.	1

Assessment

Water Works contains performance-based assessments for students to do at the beginning (preassessment) and end (postassessment) of the unit to assess learning within the unit itself. These assessments address concept attainment, scientific process/investigation, and unit content. Teachers should use the performance-based assessments results from the preassessment to adjust instructional plans for individual learners as needed. Also, the preassessments provide a baseline for determining growth as similar postassessments are administered after the unit is completed. The postassessments provide valuable information about whether students have mastered the targeted objectives and standards of learning.

An assessment on the overarching concept, change, is administered after the teacher does some preteaching. Preteaching experiences include samples of changes caused by people and samples of natural changes. Students are then given assessment templates where they are asked to draw or write about certain changes. A concept assessment rubric is used to score the change pre- and postassessments.

In the scientific investigation assessment, students are given a scientific question and are asked to design an experiment for investigating the question. A response template is given to students and this template prompts them to identify a prediction or hypothesis, materials needed for the experiment, experiment steps, data collection, and data organization for interpretation. The Science Process Skill Scoring Rubric is used to assess student's responses to the prompts.

Concept maps are used to pre- and postassess students' knowledge of water, the states of water, and the interaction of objects with water. Prior to the preassessment experience, students are taught how to create concept maps to represent their knowledge (see Appendix B). They then are given a prompt for creating a concept map about water, the states of water, and the interaction of objects with water. After creating a concept map, the student's map is awarded a specific number of points for hierarchical levels, propositions, cross-connections, and examples.

Teachers also should note that items to look for in assessment are designated in the first section of each lesson plan (under the heading, "What to Look for in Assessment"). These "look fors" are linked to the essential science understandings, scientific processes, change concept generalizations, and basic concepts that are targeted in each lesson. Teachers can develop checklists for the "look fors" or may make informal observations.

Complete assessment descriptions, directions, and scoring instructions are included in the Project Clarion Assessment Package, which is included in Appendix D.

Unit Glossary

absorb: to take in or soak up

condense: to change from a gas to a liquid

displacement: to take the place of something else

dissolve: to mix with a liquid so that the result is a liquid that is the same throughout

downhill: to move from a higher point to a lower point

evaporate: to change from a liquid to a gas

float: to rest on the surface of a liquid

flow: to move along in a stream

form: the shape or outline of a substance

freeze: to change from a liquid to a solid by cold

gas: a substance with no fixed shape that tends to expand without limit

heat: a form of energy that causes things to rise in temperature

liquid: flowing freely like water

matter: substance that occupies space, has mass, and makes up the observable universe

sink: to move downward below the surface

size: the measurements of an object

solid: a substance that keeps its size and shape

state: one of the three forms of matter such as solid, liquid, or gas

water: the liquid that descends from clouds as rain, from streams, lakes, seas, and is an odorless, tasteless compound

weight: the force with which a body is attracted toward the earth

Teacher's Guide to Content

States of Matter

All matter is made up of small particles called *atoms*. Different arrangements of atoms have different properties. Tightly compressed groups of atoms with little space between them make solid objects, whereas widely spaced groups of atoms make liquids or gasses. Three states of matter are solids, liquids, and gasses.

Each state has certain properties. A solid object keeps its shape regardless of where it is placed, is difficult to move through, and cannot be compressed. A liquid takes the shape of its container, can be moved through or poured, and only can be compressed with difficulty. A gas expands to fill its container and can be moved through and compressed easily.

Substances can move from one state to another at various temperatures. Water, for instance, has a solid form (ice), a liquid form (water), and a gaseous form (water vapor). A substance changes from solid to liquid when it reaches its melting point, from liquid to gas when it reaches it boiling point, from liquid to solid when it reaches its freezing point, and from gas to liquid when it reaches its condensation point. The melting and freezing points of any substance are the same, as are the boiling and condensation points. For water, the freezing (and melting) point is 32 °F, and the boiling (and condensation) point is 212 °F. If a substance is placed under extreme pressure, its boiling and freezing points will change.

Density

An object's mass is the amount of matter it contains. Its volume is the amount of space it fills. The more of an object you have, the more mass and volume it will have; a thimbleful of water has less matter and volume than a pond full of water. The ratio between an object's matter and volume is its density. In other words, density equals mass divided by volume. An object with a high density will have less volume than an equal mass of a less dense object. For example, a one-pound bag of feathers has a greater volume than a one-pound block of steel because the steel has the greater density.

A compound's density can be changed by changing its temperature. When a compound is heated, its atoms spread out and it expands. Because it is now taking up more volume with the same mass, its density is lower. When the compound cools and the atoms contract, it will take up less volume and its density will increase. Lava lamps work on this principle. Two substances of similar densities that will not mix together are put in the lamp. As one substance comes in contact with the lamp's heat source, it warms up and expands. Because it is now less dense than the surrounding substance, it rises to the top of the lamp. When the substance reaches the top of the lamp, it cools down, becomes denser, and sinks to the bottom. This is how the changing patterns inside the lamp are created.

Hydrodynamic Design

An object floats on water because it experiences upward pressure equal to the weight of the water it displaces. This means that in order for a boat to float, it must

9

displace an amount of water equal to its weight before it is submerged. When the boat enters the water, pressure equal to the weight of the water it displaced is applied to the bottom of the boat. This pressure forces the boat upwards and causes it to float.

Boats can be designed to improve their maneuverability using the principle of displacement. Early sailing ships had displacement hulls designed to push the water out of the way so the boat would glide smoothly through the water. Modern racing boats sometimes have a tunnel hull intended to trap a pad of water under the boat to reduce drag and increase speed.

Content Resources

International Hydrofoil Society. (n.d.). *Radical hydrofoils.* Retrieved December 14, 2005, from http://foxxaero.homestead.com/indfoil.html

Harris, T. (n.d.). *How liquid motion lamps work.* Retrieved December 14, 2005, from http://science.howstuffworks.com/lava-lamp.htm

Materials and properties. (n.d.). Retrieved December 14, 2005, from http://www.schoolscience.co.uk/content/3/chemistry/materials/match1pg1.html

Pidwirny, M. (2004). *Introduction to the hydrosphere.* Retrieved December 14, 2005, from http://www.physicalgeography.net/fundamentals/8a.html

Ophardt, C. E. (2003). *What is density?* Retrieved February 26, 2008, from http://www.elmhurst.edu/~chm/vchembook/120Adensity.html

Solids, liquids, and gases. (n.d.). Retrieved December 14, 2005, from http://www.apqj64.dsl.pipex.com/sfa/slg.htm

Why can boats made of steel float on water when a bar of steel sinks? (n.d.). Retrieved December 14, 2005, from http://science.howstuffworks.com/question254.htm

Zidock, A. (2003). *Boat hull design.* Retrieved December 14, 2005, from http://sites.state.pa.us/PA_Exec/Fish_Boat/anglerboater/1999/julaug99/boathull.htm

Teaching Resources

Required Resources

Allen, P. (1996). *Who sank the boat?* New York: The Putnam & Grosset Group.
Hewitt, S. (1998). *Forces around us.* New York: Children's Press.
Lehn, B. (1999). *What is a scientist?* Brookfield, CT: The Millbrook Press.
Morrison, G. (2006). *A drop of water.* New York: Houghton Mifflin/Walter Lorraine Books.
Wick, W. (1997). *A drop of water: A book of science and wonder.* New York: Scholastic.

Additional Resources

Broekel, R. (1988). *Experiments with water.* Chicago: Children's Press.
Cole, J., & Degan, B. (1997). *Magic school bus ups and downs: A book about floating and sinking.* New York: Scholastic.
Evans, D., & Williams, C. (1992). *Make it change.* New York: Dorling Kindersley.
Frost, H. (2000). *Water as a gas.* Mankato, MN: Pebble Books.
Frost, H. (2000). *Water as a solid.* Mankato, MN: Pebble Books.
Frost, H. (2000). *The cycle.* Mankato, MN: Pebble Books.
Richardson, J. (1992). *The water cycle.* New York: F. Watts.
Rosinsky, N. (2003). *Water: Up, down, and all around.* Minneapolis, MN: Picture Window Books.
Rowe, J. (1993). *Keep it afloat.* Chicago: Children's Press.
Stewart, M. (2006). *Will it float or sink?* Cambridge, MA: Children's Press.
Zoehfeld, K. (1998). *What is the world made of? All about solids, liquids, and gases.* New York: Harper Trophy.

Part Two: Lesson Plans

Lesson Plans

Lesson Plan Overview

Lesson 1—What Is a Scientist?

Lesson 2—What Is Change?

Lesson 3—What Scientists Do: Observe, Ask Questions, Learn More

Lesson 4—What Scientists Do: Experiment, Create Meaning, Tell Others

Lesson 5—What Are Sources of Water on Earth?

Lesson 6—Does Water Disappear?

Lesson 7—Can Water Reappear?

Lesson 8—What Happens When Water Is Mixed With Other Liquids?

Lesson 9—What Is Density?

Lesson 10—Which Things Sink and Float?

Lesson 11—Can We Make a Better Floater?

Lesson 12—What Have We Learned About Water?

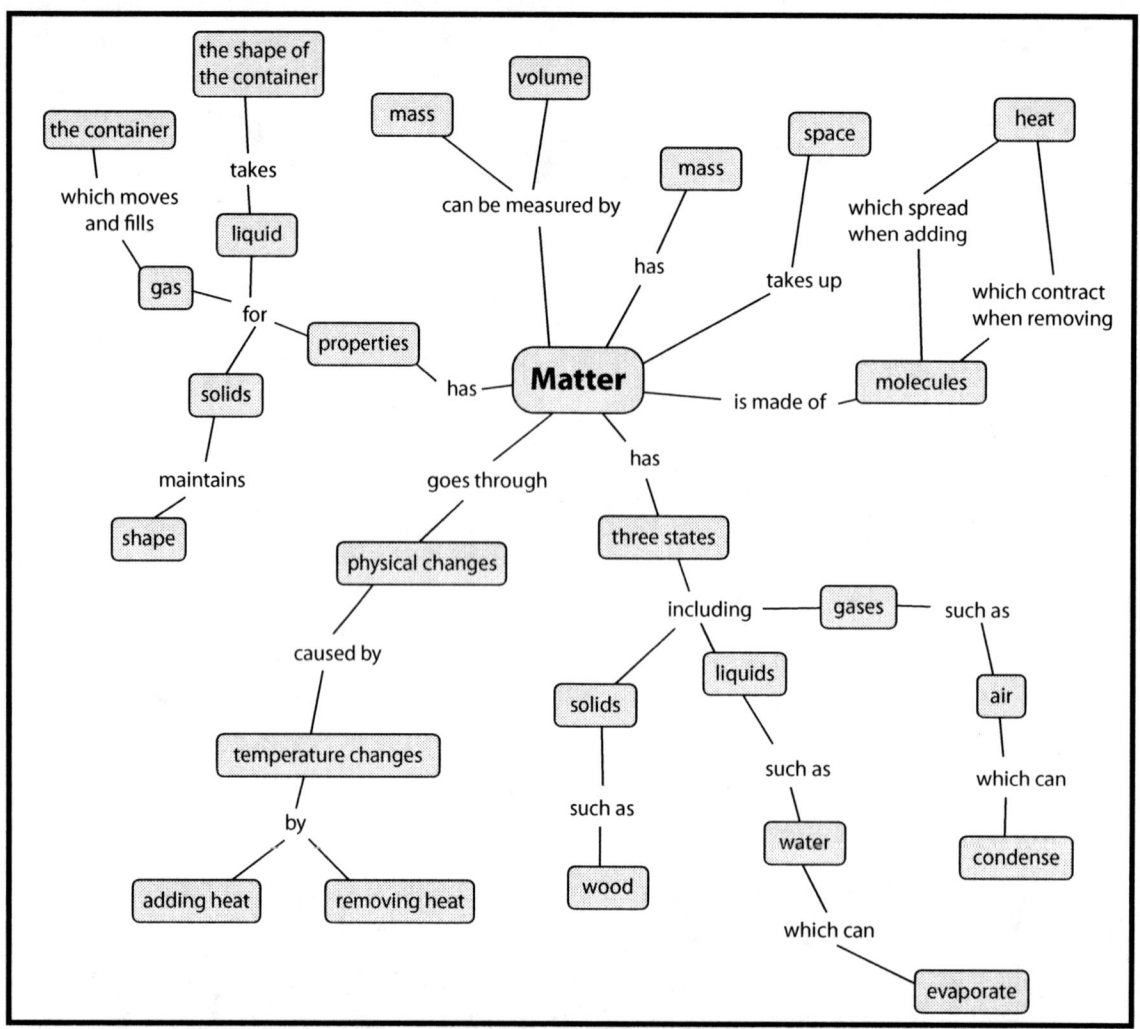

Figure 2. A concept map showing a student's understanding of matter.

Lesson Overview

The following pages provide organizational tools you can use with the lessons provided in this book. In total, 12 lessons on properties of water are included.

Unit Flowchart

The lessons in this book were designed with a particular organizational system of presenting the information in mind. Figure 2 presents a flowchart we have designed for conducting the various lessons in this unit.

Lesson Blueprint

In planning to incorporate these lessons in your classroom, you might find the blueprint included in Table 3 handy. This table breaks down each lesson, detailing the instructional purpose, essential science understandings, scientific investigations skills and processes, generalizations about the overarching concept of change, and the basic concepts emphasized in the unit.

Table 3
Lesson Breakdown for *Water Works*

Lesson #	Title	Instructional Purpose	Essential Science Understandings	Scientific Investigation Skills and Processes	Change Generalizations
	Preassessments				
1	*What Is a Scientist?*	To help students learn to recognize the specific work of scientists and the process scientists use.	• This lesson focuses on science investigation processes.	• Make observations. • Ask questions. • Learn more about observations and questions. • Design and conduct experiments. • Create meaning from the experiment. • Tell others what was found.	• Change is everywhere. • Change is related to time. • Change can be natural or manmade. • Change may be random or predictable.
2	*What Is Change?*	To deepen each student's understanding of the concept of change, by giving examples, classifying, finding nonexamples, and generalizing.	• Our five senses help us to learn more.	• Make observations. • Learn more.	• Change is everywhere. • Change is related to time. • Change can be natural or manmade. • Change may be random or predictable.
3	*What Scientists Do: Observe, Ask Questions, Learn More*	To guide students to observe, ask questions, and learn more about water.	• Senses help us to investigate scientific questions.	• Make observations. • Ask questions. • Learn more.	• Change can be natural or manmade.
4	*What Scientists Do: Experiment, Create Meaning, Tell Others*	To engage students in an investigation to create an effective water filter.	• Senses help us to investigate scientific questions.	• Conduct an experiment. • Create meaning from an experiment. • Tell others about it.	• Change may be random or predictable.
5	*What Are Sources of Water on Earth?*	To help students consider the many natural sources of water and to deepen their understanding of the movement of water.	• Water resources on the earth come in many different forms. • Water flows downhill, from a higher level to a lower level. • Water is a valuable resource that must be protected and conserved.	• Make observations. • Ask questions. • Learn more.	• Changes can be natural or manmade. • Change can be random or predictable.
6	*Does Water Disappear?*	To use the steps in the experimentation process to study. To deepen understanding of water in various states: solid, liquid, gas.	• Water can take various forms, but it is still water. • Water seems to disappear as it evaporates into the air.	• Make observations. • Make predictions. • Create record of an experiment. • Make inferences and draw conclusions.	• Change is everywhere. • Change can be natural or manmade. • Change may be perceived as orderly or random.

Lesson #	Title	Instructional Purpose	Essential Science Understandings	Scientific Investigation Skills and Processes	Change Generalizations
7	Can Water Reappear?	To use the steps in the experimentation process to study condensation. To reinforce generalizations around change. To deepen understanding of the water cycle.	• Water can take various forms, but it is still water. • Water can reappear in the form of condensation. • Condensation occurs when the temperature cools, changing water vapor into liquid.	• Make observations. • Make predictions. • Create record of an experiment. • Make inferences and draw conclusions.	• Change is everywhere. • Change can be natural or manmade. • Change may be perceived as orderly or random.
8	What Happens When Water Is Mixed With Other Liquids?	To recognize water as a solvent. To reinforce generalizations around change. To introduce the concept of density. To use data tables.	• Some liquids will separate when mixed with water. Others will not. • Some substances will dissolve in water. Others will not. • Some substances will dissolve more readily in hot water than in cold water. • Density is the relationship between an object's mass and the space it takes up.	• Make observations. • Apply prior knowledge to develop scientific explanations. • Make inferences and draw conclusions.	• Change is everywhere. • Change can be natural or manmade. • Change may be perceived as orderly or random.
9	What Is Density?	To engage students in sorting objects based on size and density and comparing the relative density of two objects.	• Our senses help us to seek, find, and react to information. • Certain objects float in water while others do not float.	• Make observations. • Ask questions. • Learn more. • Create meaning.	• Change is everywhere. • Change may be random or predictable.
10	Which Things Sink or Float?	To engage students in an exploration of the concept of density and in predicting which things will sink and which will float.	• Water can be a solid, liquid, or gas. • Certain objects float in water while others do not float..	• Design and conduct an experiment.	• Change can be natural or manmade. • Change can be orderly or random.
11	Can We Make a Better Floater?	Students learn about displacement and design clay boats to hold more weight.	• Water can be a solid, liquid, or gas. • Certain objects float in water while other do not float.	• Design and conduct an experiment.	• Change can be examined orderly or random.
12	What Have We Learned About Water?	To engage students in a review of what they have learned, giving examples of something they did in class that matches change generalizations, scientific processes, and essential content learning.	• Water can be a solid, liquid, or gas. • The state of water changes by heating or cooling. • Water evaporates into the air. • Water condenses on cold surfaces. • Some liquids will separate when mixed with water. • Some substances will dissolve in water while others will not. • Certain objects float in water while others do not float. • Some solids dissolve in water and others do not.	• Create meaning. • Tell others what was found.	• Change is everywhere. • Change can be natural or manmade. • Change can be perceived as orderly or random. • Change relates to time.

Lesson 1: What Is a Scientist?

Planning the Lesson

Instructional Purpose: To learn the characteristics of scientists and investigation skills that scientists use.

Instructional Time: 45 minutes

Essential Science Understandings:
- This lesson focuses on science investigation processes.

Scientific Investigation Skills and Processes:
- Make observations.
- Ask questions.
- Learn more about observations and questions.
- Design and conduct experiments.
- Create meaning from the experiments.
- Tell others what was found from the experiments.

What to Look for in Assessment:
- Can the student distinguish between scientists and nonscientists?
- Can the student identify scientific investigation processes used by scientists?

Materials/Resources/Equipment:
- Lab coat for the teacher
- Student "lab coats" (optional; could use one white T-shirt or dress shirt for each student)
- Beaker
- Microscope
- Prepared charts or transparencies of A Scientist Is . . . handout on p. 19
- Copies of the Pictures of People handouts (see p 20–21)
- Marker
- One lab log for each student
- The Wheel of Scientific Investigation and Reasoning poster (see p. 22)
- One piece of chart paper
- *What Is a Scientist?* by B. Lehn, published by The Millbrook Press

Teacher's Note: Scientific investigation is introduced to the students in three lessons: Lesson 1, Lesson 3, and Lesson 4. The processes introduced in these lessons are applied throughout the unit.

Implementing the Lesson

1. Put on a lab coat and pick up a beaker and microscope. Ask the students what kind of job you might have. Explain that you are a *scientist*. Ask the students if they know a scientist and allow them to discuss what they know about scientists or their experiences with scientists. Questions to ask include:
    a. Do you know a scientist?
    b. What do you think scientists do?

2. Define a scientist as, "a person who studies nature and the physical world by testing, experimenting, and measuring" (Scholastic, 1996; see A Scientist Is . . . handout on p. 19). Show the students the Pictures of People handouts (pp. 20–21). Tell students to look for clues to sort the pictures according to whether the person is a scientist or not. Help students apply the definition in sorting the pictures into two groups: (1) Scientists and (2) Not Scientists. Questions to ask include:
    a. What clues might tell you that someone is a scientist?
    b. Describe why you think the person probably is or is not a scientist.

3. Ask the students what they think scientists do and write down their responses on chart paper. Display The Wheel of Scientific Investigation and Reasoning (see p. 22). Read the wheel to the students and talk about what each item means. Ask the students to compare the wheel's processes with the list the class created.

4. Show students the book *What Is a Scientist?* by Barbara Lehn. Ask students to look for what scientists do while you are reading the book. Read the book, showing the pictures to the students and pointing out the clues that will help students understand what a scientist does. As you read each page, relate the activity to the scientific investigation processes included on the wheel. Ask students these questions:
    a. What did the scientists do in the book?
    b. What makes someone a scientist?
    c. When is someone *not* a scientist?

5. Explain that the students will be working as scientists in the unit. Have students put on their lab coats. Explain to the students that they are going to learn to think like a scientist and learn how to do what scientists do.

6. Tell students that scientists keep a scientific investigation log of what they are doing. They date the pages in their logs and then write down what they have learned or what they are thinking about what they have learned. Tell students that they are going to keep a log and they are going to make the first page. Ask each student to date the first page and to draw a picture of him- or herself investigating something. Give students the following instructions:
    a. Draw yourself being a scientist. What would you investigate/study/do?

7. Have students share their completed pictures with the class.
8. Concluding Questions/Activities:
    a. Would you like to be a scientist? Why or why not?
    b. All science is about how things stay the same and how they change. How do scientists study change?

Extending the Lesson

- Set up a learning center where students can cut out pictures from magazines, the newspaper, etc., of people who are scientists and paste the pictures on a class collage.
- Provide props and lab coats for students to role-play being a scientist in the housekeeping section of the classroom.
- Provide books of individuals who are investigating something in the library center of the classroom.

What to Do at Home
- Ask students to ask their parent or some other adult to respond to the question, "What would you investigate/study/do if you were a scientist?"

Name:_____ Date:_____

A Scientist Is . . .

A scientist is someone who . . .

studies nature and the physical world by testing, experimenting, and measuring.

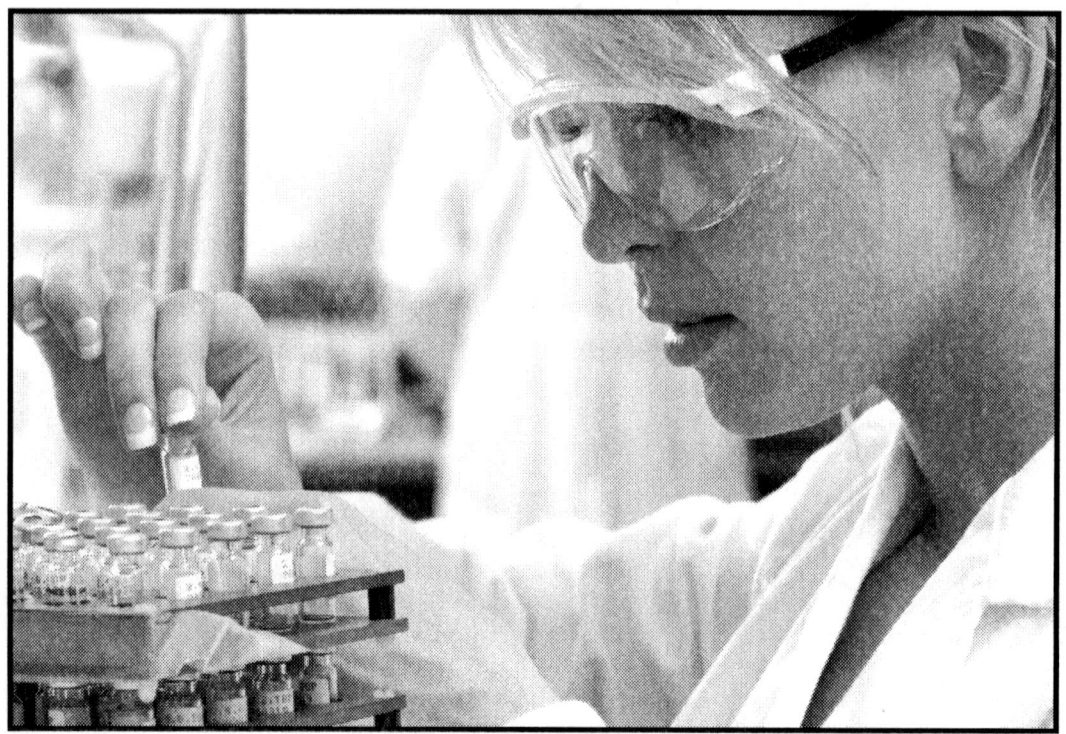

Scientists . . .

try to find answers to questions they have about our world. Often, they improve our world by finding answers to their questions.

Name:_____ Date:_____

Pictures of People

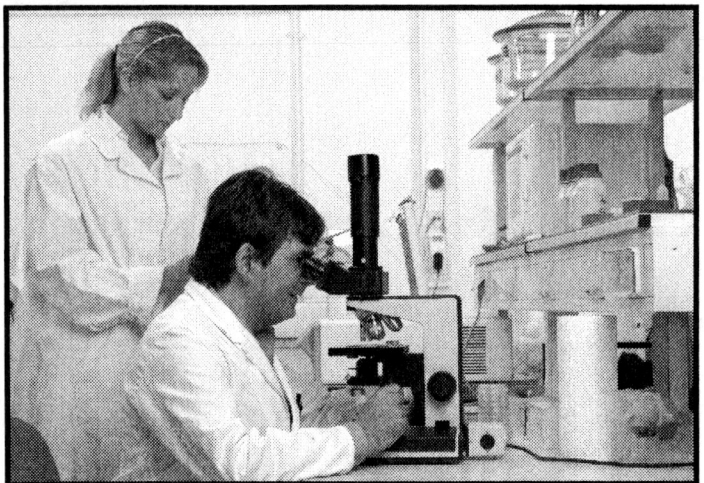

© Prufrock Press Inc. • *Water Works*
This page may be photocopied or reproduced with permission for classroom use only.

Name:_____ Date:_____

Pictures of People

Name:_____ Date:_____

What Scientists Do:
The Wheel of Scientific Investigation and Reasoning

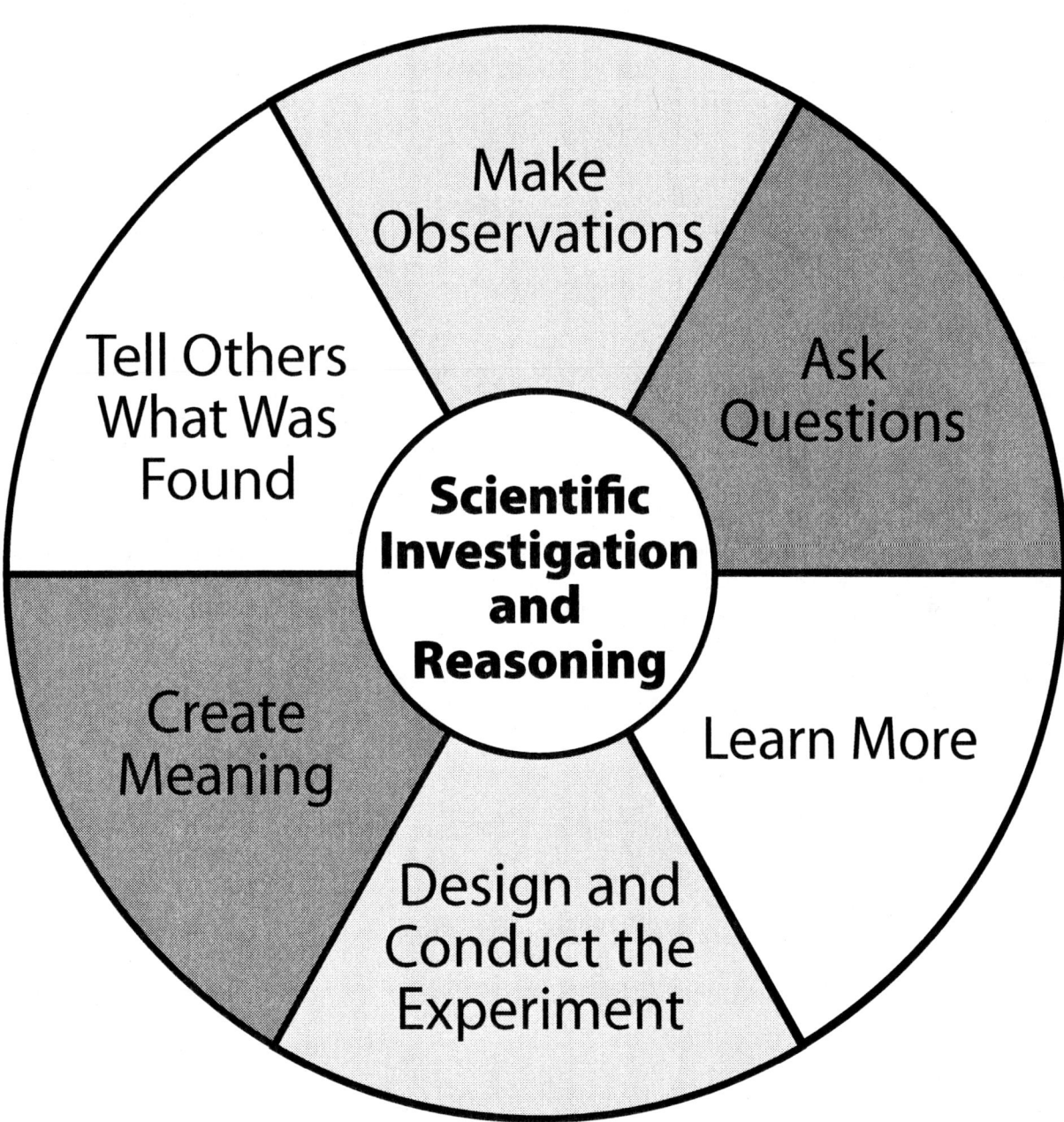

Lesson 2: What Is Change?

Planning the Lesson

Instructional Purpose: To deepen each student's understanding of the concept of change, by giving examples, classifying, finding nonexamples, and generalizing.

Instructional Time: 45 minutes

Essential Science Understandings:
- Our five senses help us to learn more.

Scientific Investigation Skills and Processes:
- Make observations.
- Learn more.

Concept Generalizations:
- Change is everywhere.
- Change is related to time.
- Change can be natural or manmade.
- Change may be random or predictable.

What to Look for in Assessment:
- Can students provide examples of change?
- Can students categorize examples of change, explaining their reasoning?
- Can students show understanding of the concept of generalization?
- Can students provide an example for a change generalization?

Materials/Resources/Equipment:
- Five Senses Chart (see p. 26)
- Popcorn (popped and unpopped)
- Garlic salt
- Four sentence strips with a different change generalization written on each strip
- Chart paper
- Change Is Everywhere handout (see p. 27)

Implementing the Lesson

1. Tell students they are going to explore a concept that is important to understanding our world—*change*. Explain that scientists spend a lot of time either trying to explain why a change occurred or causing a change to occur. Ask students how scientists study change.
2. Explain that scientists often study change using their senses. Ask students to name the five senses. Post the Five Senses Chart (see p. 26) in your classroom. Perform the

Teacher's Notes:
- Some nonexamples of change include gravity and the past.
- Post a chart with the change generalizations in the classroom.

23

following tasks to demonstrate the different ways that change can be observed and write student observations on the chart.
- a. Show students some unpopped popcorn kernels. Ask students to describe the kernels only by looking at them. What do they *see*?
- b. Rip a popped kernel in half. Ask students to describe how the popcorn changed. What sense first detected the change? Ask students questions such as,
    - i. Did you use your ears?
    - ii. Did you hear anything?
- c. Next, pass around popped popcorn. Ask students to smell it and to describe the *smell* of the popcorn. Ask students to rip the popcorn in half. How did the popcorn change?
- d. Have the students close their eyes. Sprinkle garlic salt on the popcorn and let students smell it again with their eyes closed. Tell students to open their eyes. Can they *see* a change? How did they know there was a change?
- e. Have a volunteer *taste* the popcorn and describe it to the class. Ask students how they could make the taste of the popcorn change.
- f. Let each student *feel* the popcorn. Flatten the popcorn between your fingers and pass it around. Have them feel and describe the change.

3. Caution students that scientists have to be careful when using certain senses to determine change because their senses could be harmed. Ask students to provide examples of how using a certain sense to determine a change might be harmful. (Mention allergies, as well as other safety concerns.)
4. Display the Taba Concept Model chart (Table 4) for the class (the class will be filling in several of the sections of the chart as this lesson progresses).

Table 4
Taba Concept Model Chart

Examples of Change	Categories of Change
Nonexamples of Change	Generalizations About Change

5. Ask students to draw an example of change and to share their drawings at their table.
6. Discuss what it means to classify things. Model the classification of objects into different categories using several of the basic concepts as possible categories. Remind students that in order to classify objects, they must find some way in which the objects are similar. Suggest that one category might be *people*. Ask students to bring up their drawing to the front of the room if it matched the category. Tape up the examples. Ask students to think of another category and continue the process of taping up the categories until all the drawn examples of change have been taped.
7. Ask students to think about things that do not change. Can they come up with an idea of something that does not change? If this is difficult, suggest that they ask their parents this evening to see if they can think of something that does not change.
8. Discuss as a class why it was easier to think of examples of change.
9. Explain that scientists often generalize or make statements about how examples are similar and these generalizations help scientists understand our world. Ask students what they know about change by looking at the examples and nonexamples. Provide the students one example as a model (i.e., "I notice that there are many different kinds of changes" or "Everything changes"). Write down your statement on the section of the class chart labeled "Generalizations."
10. Present the following generalizations by posting sentence strips in the section of the class chart labeled "Generalizations" and explain to students that they will be looking at how these generalizations help scientists understand change. Ask students to talk about each one and give some examples.
    a. Change is everywhere.
    b. Change is related to time.
    c. Change can be natural or manmade.
    d. Change can be random or predictable.

11. Discuss with students how the popcorn examples apply to the change generalizations. Model by saying that the popcorn examples showed that change relates to time (i.e., "I noticed some time went by in order for the popcorn to change"). Question the children in order for them to relate the generalizations to the popcorn experiment. ("The change was manmade because you put it into the microwave.")
12. Concluding Questions/Activities:
    a. What change can you make right now in how you look?
    b. What is one change that will happen when winter comes?
    c. How does the weather change?

Extending the Lesson

Journal Questions and/or Prompts
- I like change because . . .
- I do not like change because . . .

What to Do at Home
- Change Is Everywhere handout (see p. 27)

Name: _____ Date: _____

Five Senses Chart

Sight				
Sound				
Smell				
Touch				
Taste				

© **Prufrock Press Inc.** • *Water Works*

This page may be photocopied or reproduced with permission for classroom use only.

Name: _____   Date: _____

Draw and label four things that change in your house.

Change Is Everywhere

Lesson 3: What Scientists Do: Observe, Ask Questions, Learn More

Planning the Lesson

Instructional Purposes: To apply three of six investigation processes (make observations, ask questions, and learn more) described in The Wheel of Scientific Investigation and Reasoning; to initiate an investigation of water.

Instructional Time: 45 minutes

Essential Science Understandings:
- This lesson focuses on scientific investigation processes.

Scientific Investigation Skills and Processes:
- Make observations.
- Ask questions.
- Learn more about observations and questions.

Change Concept Generalizations:
- Change can be natural or manmade.

What to Look for in Assessment:
- The student can apply the steps of scientific investigation.

Materials/Resources/Equipment:
- Student lab coats (optional)
- Chart paper
- Large clear plastic container of muddy water
- Chart, poster, or transparency of The Wheel of Scientific Investigation and Reasoning (see p. 22)
- Copies of the Water Observations chart for each student (see p. 31)
- Students' lab logs
- 1 small clear plastic container of muddy water and 1 small clear plastic container of clean water per group of 3–4 students

Implementing the Lesson

1. Have students put on their lab coats. Explain to students that they are going to learn to think and work like a scientist using the scientific investigation processes.
2. Ask students to share their parents' responses to the prompt from the homework assigned in Lesson 1: What would you investigate/do if you were a scientist?
3. Ask students what they think it means when we say that scientists "investigate" something. Explain that to investigate something means that you find out as much as you can about it. You might use the following prompts:
   a. Tell me whether you have ever investigated something.

b. What did you investigate?
   c. How did you investigate it?

4. Use the The Wheel of Scientific Investigation and Reasoning (p. 22) to review the six processes introduced in Lesson 1 and explain that scientists do these things to "investigate" or learn about something: (1) make observations, (2) ask questions, (3) learn more about observations and questions, (4) design and conduct experiments, (5) create meaning, and (6) tell others what was found in the experiments. Remind students that scientists use these processes when learning about their world.

5. Point to the Make Observations section on the wheel. Tell students that the first thing scientists do is use their senses to learn about something. Describe the senses and the body part associated with each of the senses. Explain to the class that they are going to use their senses to observe water. Tell students, "For today's and tomorrow's lessons, we are going to pretend that we have been stranded on a deserted island." Ask students the following question: If you were stranded on a deserted island, what is something you could not survive without?

6. Post student responses on a piece of chart paper. (Hopefully students will come up with water as a critical need. If not, then prompt students to arrive at this response.) Following the identification of water as a critical need, tell students, "Now imagine that after wandering around, you have stumbled upon a small pond of muddy water." Show students a clear plastic container filled with muddy water. Ask them: Do you want to drink this water? Why not?

7. Tell students that because they are learning to think and solve problems like scientists do, their task is going to be to practice the processes that are shown on the wheel. Prompting questions could include: When you make observations, you use your senses to learn. What sense do you use most to make observations?

8. Divide students into groups of 3–4. Give each group a clear, small container of muddy water and a clear, small container of clean water. Tell them that they will make observations of the containers of muddy water and record their observations on the Water Observations handout (p. 31). Explain to the students that they will use their senses to make observations about the water. Distribute the handout and remind students that it is not safe to use all of their senses for all experiments. Tell them, "The square to record responses for Taste has been grayed out because it is not safe for you to taste the muddy water. You are to write words that describe the muddy water based on what you observe." When they have had time to complete their work, ask students: What senses did you use to make observations about the water?

9. Tell students that now they will have a chance to put their skills of question-asking to work. Point to the Ask Questions section on the wheel. Have students think about questions they could ask about the muddy water. Ask students: What questions do you have about the water? Prompt students by reminding them that they need this water to survive on their deserted island.

10. Record their responses on a piece of chart paper. If the students are hesitant, the teacher should give an example of a question he or she has to encourage students. Help students understand the difference between making a statement and asking a question. If students make a statement, rephrase the statement as a question. Write down the students' questions on chart paper. Then model your questions, recording them on the board, overhead, or chart paper, such as:

   a. How might we use this muddy water to survive?
   b. What are some ways that we could try to make the water clean?

11. Point to the Learn More section of the wheel. Ask students how they can gather information to learn more and encourage them to think of the many ways people learn. Emphasize that the more they observe something, the more they can learn about it. Ask students what they noticed about the muddy water:
    a. How is the muddy water like clear water? How is it different?
    b. What questions do you have about water that are not already on our list?
    c. When you want to learn more about something, what do you do?

12. Review the Scientific Investigation Process Skills that you covered today: Make Observations, Ask Questions, and Learn More.
13. Tell students that they are going to learn more about water through investigation. Have students open their lab logs and either draw or write about their observations of water.
14. Guide students to draw conclusions about their findings. Ask them if they can describe the differences between clear water and muddy water using their senses to guide them.
15. Concluding Questions/Activities:
    a. Describe some things scientists do when they want to answer a scientific question.
    b. What do you know about water?
    c. What questions do you have about water?

Extending the Lesson

What to Do at Home
- Ask students to look for ways that water is used in their home and bring drawings or a word list of what they find.

Name:_____ Date:_____

Water Observations

Sight	
Sound	
Smell	
Touch	
Taste	

Lesson 4:
What Scientists Do: Experiment, Create Meaning, Tell Others

Planning the Lesson

Instructional Purposes: To design and conduct an experiment using water; to create meaning from the experiment; to learn how to tell others what was found.

Instructional Time: 45 minutes

Essential Science Understandings:
- This lesson focuses on scientific investigation processes.

Scientific Investigation Skills and Processes:
- Design and conduct an experiment.
- Create meaning.
- Tell others what was found in the experiment.

Change Concept Generalizations:
- Change may be random or predictable.

What to Look for in Assessment:
- Can students design and conduct an experiment?
- Can students interpret data from a data table?
- Can students describe how the experiment was conducted and what results were found?

Materials/Resources/Equipment:
- Student lab coats (optional)
- The Wheel of Scientific Investigation and Reasoning poster (p. 22)
- One 2-liter soda bottle cut in half per group of 3–4 students
- Rubber bands
- Copies of A Hypothesis Is . . . handout on p. 35 for each student
- Chart or transparency of Steps for Our Water Experiment handout on p. 36
- Student lab logs
- Items for filtration, including cotton balls, gravel, sand, charcoal, paper coffee filter, cheese cloth, and/or nylon stockings—enough for each group to select more than one agent for filtration
- Copies of student badges on p. 37 (enough for each student to receive a badge)

Implementing the Lesson

1. Ask students to share their findings from doing the homework assignment, asking, In what ways is water used in your home?

2. Review what the class did during the previous lesson (Lesson 3), using the following questions:
   a. What did we start investigating in our last lesson?
   b. What did we do to begin our investigation of water?
   c. What did we observe about water?
   d. What questions did we have about water?

3. Introduce the lesson with the following: "In the last lesson, we began an investigation of muddy water to practice making observations, asking questions, and learning more. Today, we will continue thinking like scientists, and we will design and conduct an experiment to solve our water problem." Have students put on their lab coats.

4. Tell students that they are going to engage in an activity to solve our muddy water problem in order to help them learn to design and conduct experiments. Remind students that their problem is that they need clean water to drink because they are stranded on a deserted island, and the only water they have is muddy. They will use the scientific method to try to solve their problem.

5. Point to the wheel's Design and Conduct the Experiment section. Note that the first things scientists do to conduct an experiment is to form a hypothesis from their question or questions. Use the handout on p. 35 to define hypothesis as *a temporary prediction that can be tested about how a scientific investigation or experiment will turn out*. Explain to the students that they are going to design and conduct an experiment to answer the question: "How can we make this muddy water clean?" Tell students they will form a hypothesis.

6. Show students the possible filtering agents (Group A: cotton balls, gravel, sand, charcoal, paper coffee filter; Group B: cheese cloth, nylon stocking). Instruct students that they will select two items from Group A and one item from Group B to create their water filter. Their hypothesis will be based on the items selected to act as a filter.

7. Explain that the hypothesis needs to be tested. Ask students what they think "to test a hypothesis" means. Then, encourage students to share how they think the class could find out whether the prediction or hypothesis was true, by asking, "How do you think we could find out whether our prediction or hypothesis is true?"

8. *Note to Teacher:* The filter is created by the following process: The soda bottles should be cut in half prior to the start of class to save time. You can use both the top and the bottom of the bottles to conduct the experiment. The cheese cloth or nylon stocking is used over the mouth of the bottle and secured with the rubber band. The other two filtration items are placed in the open end of the bottle to create the filter. The muddy water is poured from the small clear plastic container and can be caught in the other half of the soda bottle.

9. Explain that it is important to plan the experiment by listing the steps. Ask students to tell what steps they would take. After students share, reveal the list of steps the class is going to follow (see p. 36). Point out the list of materials that are needed for the experiment.

10. Allow students to work in small groups to experiment with their water filters. Ask them to compare their filtered water with that of other groups. Tell students to record their findings in their lab logs. (*Note:* You may need to discuss how to create a data table to record findings.) Findings should answer these questions:
    a. Which filter created the cleanest water?
    b. Which filter left the water the muddiest?

11. Now ask students what they have discovered. Discuss their findings.

12. Ask students to do their experiment again. Explain to the students that it is important for them to confirm their findings or show that they found the same thing when they conducted the experiment a second time.
13. After all of the data have been recorded, ask students to think about what the data mean and answer the question, What are the best items for water filtration? By doing this, explain that they are creating meaning, another section of the wheel.
14. Tell students that they have just conducted an experiment. They tested their hypothesis and now they need to tell others what they found out. Point to the final section of The Wheel of Scientific Investigation and Reasoning: Tell Others What Was Found.
15. Ask students how they could share this new information with other people. Allow students to think about and talk about ways to do this. Tell students that they could tell people, they could draw pictures, and so forth.
16. Proclaim that the student scientists have just conducted an experiment and give out badges to each student to celebrate their success (see p. 37). Also, ask students to date and make the following entry in their lab logs: Draw a picture of your group conducting the water experiment we did today when acting like scientists.
17. Concluding Questions/Activities:
    a. What are the best items for water filtration?
    b. What sense(s) did you use to decide which water filter was most effective?
    c. Why do scientists try things many times?
    d. Explain how we acted like scientists today. What were the steps we did for the experiment?
    e. Why do you think scientists do experiments?

Extending the Lesson

- Create the ultimate water filter using all of the water filtration materials. Conduct a demonstration for the students. Is it more effective to use all of the materials? What would be the pros and cons of this?

What to Do at Home
- Ask students to check at home and see what kind, if any, water filtration devices or systems that their parents use or have in place.

Name:_____ Date:_____

A Hypothesis Is . . .

a temporary prediction that can be tested about how a scientific investigation or experiment will turn out.

Name:_____ Date:_____

Steps for Our Water Experiment

Hypothesis: We think that _____

and _____ with

_____ will give us the cleanest water.

Experiment Steps:

- Step 1: Gather materials.
- Step 2: Create the water filter.
- Step 3: Test the hypothesis.
- Step 3: Record what happened.
- Step 4: Try it again.
- Step 5: Record what happened.

Materials Needed:

- Small container of muddy water
- One 2-liter soda bottle cut in half per group of 3–4 students
- Items for filtration: cotton balls, gravel, sand, charcoal, paper coffee filter, cheese cloth, nylon stocking
- Pencils

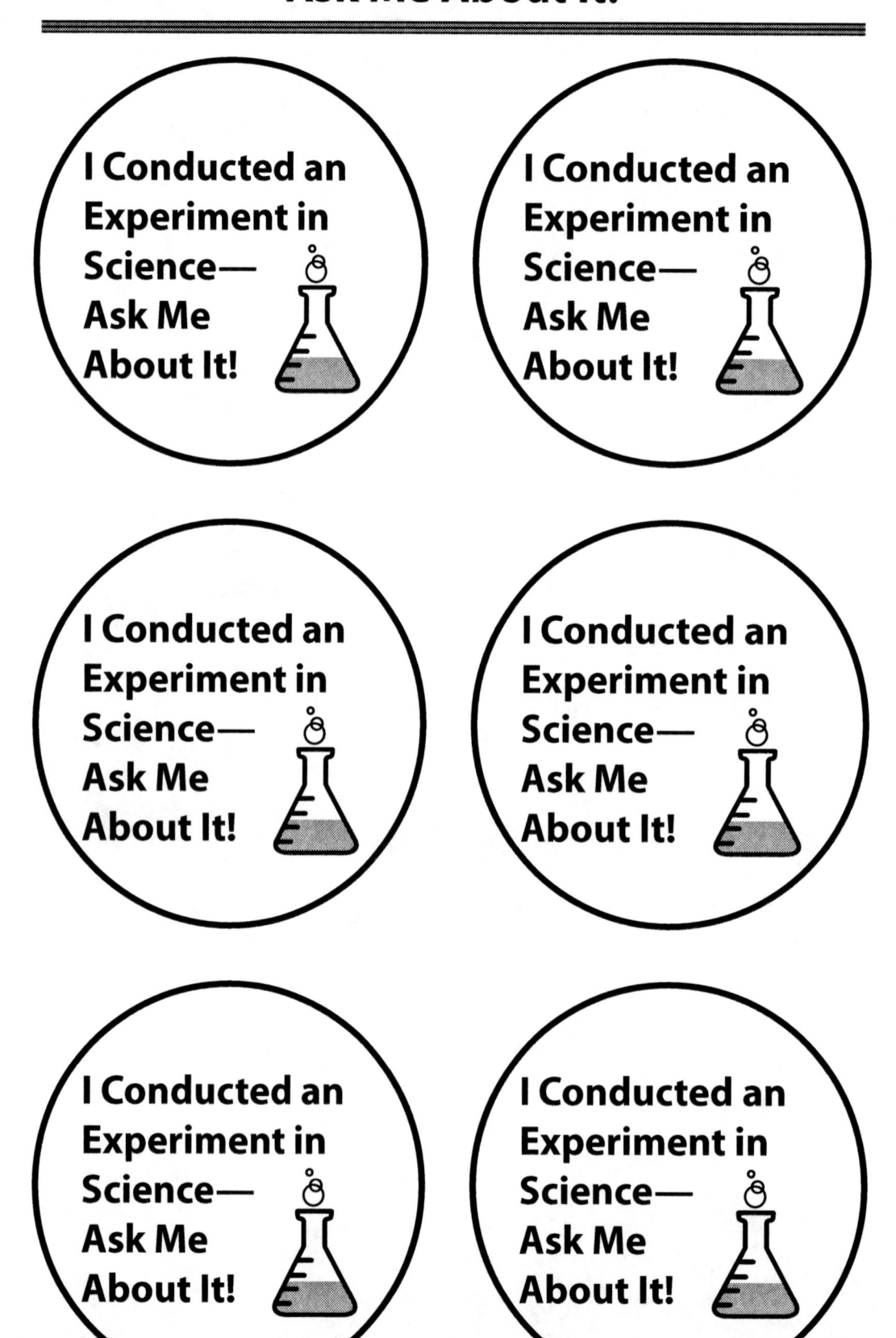

I Conducted an Experiment in Science— Ask Me About It!

I Conducted an Experiment in Science— Ask Me About It!

I Conducted an Experiment in Science— Ask Me About It!

I Conducted an Experiment in Science— Ask Me About It!

I Conducted an Experiment in Science— Ask Me About It!

I Conducted an Experiment in Science— Ask Me About It!

I Conducted an Experiment in Science— Ask Me About It!

© Prufrock Press Inc. • *Water Works*
This page may be photocopied or reproduced with permission for classroom use only.

Lesson 5:
What Are Sources of Water on Earth?

Planning the Lesson

Instructional Purposes: To help students consider the many natural sources of water; to deepen their understanding of the movement of water.

Instructional Time: 45 minutes

Essential Science Understandings:
- Water resources on the earth come in many different forms.
- Water flows downhill, from a higher level to a lower level.
- Water is a valuable resource that must be protected and conserved.

Scientific Investigation Skills and Processes:
- Make Observations.
- Ask Questions.
- Learn More.

Change Concept Generalizations:
- Changes can be natural or manmade.
- Change can be random or predictable.

What to Look for in Assessment:
- Can students name different sources of water?
- Can students describe types of movement?
- Can students suggest different ways to conserve water?

Materials/Resources/Equipment:
- Simulated landscapes (one simulating mountainous land and one simulating land with gentle ridges and valleys)
- Water
- Large plastic tub
- Chart paper
- Newspaper
- Plastic wrap
- Clay and plastic figures, small rocks, etc. (optional)
- *A Drop of Water* by G. Morrison, published by Houghton Mifflin/Walter Lorraine Books

Teacher's Note: Create a simulated landscape in a plastic tub. Use crumpled newspapers covered in plastic wrap to simulate the flow of water downhill, as well as the formation of puddles. You also may use clay and various plastic objects to further simulate the environment.

Implementing the Lesson

1. Show several picture cards of various landscapes, asking students to look for evidence of water in each one of them. Ask students to identify the various landforms shown in the pictures.

2. Tell students that water comes from many different sources. Ask them to name various sources as you list them on chart paper (e.g., oceans, rivers, lakes). Ask students to share what they know about the various water sources. Next, ask students if they have ever seen a waterfall (e.g., Niagara Falls, other natural waterfalls, waterfall at a pool, amusement park). Ask students to describe how the water flows.
3. Demonstrate the flow of water from a cup into a larger container. Does the water flow in the same direction?
4. Show students the simulated landscapes. Ask students to describe what they see. (Alternatively, ask students to help you create a landscape in which water will move in different ways).
5. Next, ask several students to take turns pouring water onto the landscapes, starting from the higher end of the landscape.
6. Remind students that scientists make predictions to learn more about different things. In this case, ask students to make a prediction about how the water will flow. Ask the class to talk about what is happening to the water:
    a. What observations and predictions have you made about water?
    b. How does it move?
    c. Does it change size or shape?
    d. How does the water flow?
    e. Can you make the water go uphill?
    f. Can you give an example of water you have seen that flows downhill? (Puddle, water slide, stream, etc.)

7. Help students to conclude that water flows downhill, from a higher level to a lower level. Have students draw pictures of water in nature, showing water flowing from high places downhill to lower places.
8. Read students the book, *A Drop of Water*, by Gordon Morrison. This book traces a drop of water through the water cycle.
9. Concluding Questions/Activities:
    a. Ask students to tell what happened in the book to the first drop of water. Using, the terms *condensation* and *evaporation,* talk about the journey of the water. Tell students that in the next lesson they will explore condensation and evaporation in scientific investigations, just like scientists do. They will consider how water can change from one form to another.

Extending the Lesson

- Set up a learning center to include water vocabulary words and pictures to match.
- Provide students with materials to create a landscape and use cups of water to demonstrate the flow of water downhill.
- Ask students to help you create a water sources picture collection for the center. Students may use the pictures to talk about the flow of water and to create sentences, stories, and booklets about water sources.

Lesson 6: Does Water Disappear?

Planning the Lesson

Instructional Purposes: To use the steps in the experimentation process to study evaporation; to deepen an understanding of water in various states: solid, liquid, gas.

Instructional Time: 45 minutes

Essential Science Understandings:
- Water can take various forms, but it is still water.
- Water seems to disappear as it evaporates into the air.

Scientific Investigation Skills and Processes:
- Make observations.
- Make predictions.
- Create a record of an experiment.
- Make inferences and draw conclusions.

Change Concept Generalizations:
- Change is everywhere.
- Change can be natural or manmade.
- Change may be perceived as orderly or random.

What to Look for in Assessment:
- Can students make a prediction?
- Can students describe what happens to water as it evaporates?
- Can students record predictions and experiment steps?

Materials/Resources/Equipment:
- Student lab coats (optional)
- Plastic clear cups
- Markers
- Solid, liquid, gas labels
- *A Drop of Water: A Book of Science and Wonder* by W. Wick, published by Scholastic
- Chart paper
- Saucers
- Measuring cups
- Water, ice
- Plastic zipper bags
- Copies of the Disappearing Water Concept Map and Disappearing Water Concept Map Word Bank handouts on pp. 44–45
- The Wheel of Scientific Investigation and Reasoning poster on p. 22
- Student lab logs

Implementing the Lesson

1. Put on lab coats and remind students that today they will try to think like scientists do. Explain that they will use some of the ways scientists work, including the following:
   a. One way scientists work to answer their questions is to observe. They do this carefully so that they can compare what they observe to what others observe.
   b. Your observation skills are improved when you take the time to look for all of the details and use as many senses as you can.

2. Show students water in different forms (cup of ice, cup of water, cup of very hot water). Ask students to observe the differences in the three cups and to describe what they see. Record student responses on chart.

3. Ask students what each cup contains. (Water). Tell students that these cups provide them an opportunity to see water in three different states: solid, liquid, and gas. Invite students to consider which label (solid, liquid, gas) goes with each cup and ask volunteers to place the labels in front of the cups. Explain that the hot cup of water is emitting steam, which is a gas. Remind students that this steam is very hot, and that they should not go near steam here or in their kitchen.

4. Ask students to think about the ways in which water can change states.
   a. How does water change from liquid to solid?
   b. How does water change from liquid to gas?
   c. How does water change from solid to liquid?
   d. Is the solid still water?
   e. Is the gas still water?

5. Next, tell students that all of these changes happen naturally. Ask students to think of examples in nature where water changes states because of nature. Record examples on chart paper. Then ask students to give you examples of manmade changes of water. Record these examples.

6. Ask students if they think that water stays the same in any ways when it changes from solid to liquid. Allow all responses to be considered and record these. Provide each student with a plastic bag filled with two ice cubes. Ask students to make a prediction related to time.
   a. What will happen to the ice cubes over time?
   b. Can you think of other things that might react in the same way?
   c. What about the color of the ice? Will it change over time?
   d. What about the texture? Will it change over time?
   e. What about the shape?
   f. What are some other examples of frozen water?
   g. What makes the ice change to liquid?

7. Collect the bags of ice. Ask students to draw in their lab logs a prediction of what will happen to the ice cubes over time. Tell students to label their drawings.

8. Refer students to The Wheel of Scientific Investigation and Reasoning. Remind students that they know quite a bit about water. Remind them about their discussions on water cycles, the ways a drop of water can change (refer back to the reading of *A Drop of Water* in the previous lesson), and the natural sources of water. Refer to the Design and Conduct the Experiment section, telling students that today they will experiment with water to see if they can make it disappear.

9. Place students into groups of 3 or 4, providing each group with a saucer, a measuring cup, a small cup, and a marker for marking the level on the cup. Tell students to draw a line on the cup with the marker. Pour water into the cup up to the mark and then pour the water into the saucer. Leave the saucer in a warm place overnight. After some time, ask the students to pour the water back into the cup to see if it is still up to the level marked on the cup.
10. Help students to make a class record of this experiment, recording the question, the predictions, the steps in the experiment, and the information (data) they will collect. Leave room on the chart to record their findings and conclusions.
11. Tell students to make a prediction for the level of the water over time. Will it stay the same, go higher than the mark, or go lower than the mark? Students should record their predictions in their lab logs. Leave the water for several hours or overnight. Then ask students to observe and record in their lab logs what happened to each of the dishes of water.
    a. Do the dishes of water look the same?
    b. What happened over time?
    c. Why did this happen?

12. Using the class chart developed earlier, record the class findings and their conclusions. Explain to students that the word used for the process of water disappearing into the air is *evaporation*. Ask students for examples of evaporation they have seen in their lives (puddles, drops of water on the counter, dried up lakes, ponds, hair drying, clothes drying).
    a. What does evaporation mean?
    b. What are the different states of water when it changes?
    c. What causes evaporation?

13. Ask students if they can think of a way to speed up evaporation. Make a list of possibilities. Ask students to choose which possibility is most likely to work (heat). Conduct a demonstration using a wet paper towel and a hair dryer, asking students to explain the process of evaporation. Explain to students that the water actually changes into invisible water vapor that mixes with the air.
14. Concluding Questions/Activities:
    a. Share some parts of the book, *A Drop of Water: A Book of Science and Wonder*, by Walter Wick to reinforce the concepts of states of matter, water sources, the water cycle, and evaporation. *Note that this book is different from the book used in the previous lesson.*
    b. Provide students with copies of the Disappearing Water Concept Map and Word Bank, pages 44–45, to reinforce the major concepts of this lesson. Encourage students to complete the map with a partner. Ask the following questions prior to completing the concept maps.
        i. Can water change from one form to another?
        ii. Is it still water when it changes?
        iii. What are the different states of water called?
        iv. When ice changes to water, it changes from a ____ to a ____.
        v. What are the different states of water?
        vi. What causes water to seem to disappear into the air?

Extending the Lesson

- Add simple materials to the water center in the classroom to allow students to experiment with disappearing (evaporating) water. For example, students can

see how long it takes for an ice cube to evaporate under different conditions (temperature, container).
- Encourage students to explain the term *evaporate* to their family. Ask students to talk about why evaporation might be positive or negative.

Name: _____ Date: _____

Disappearing Water Concept Map

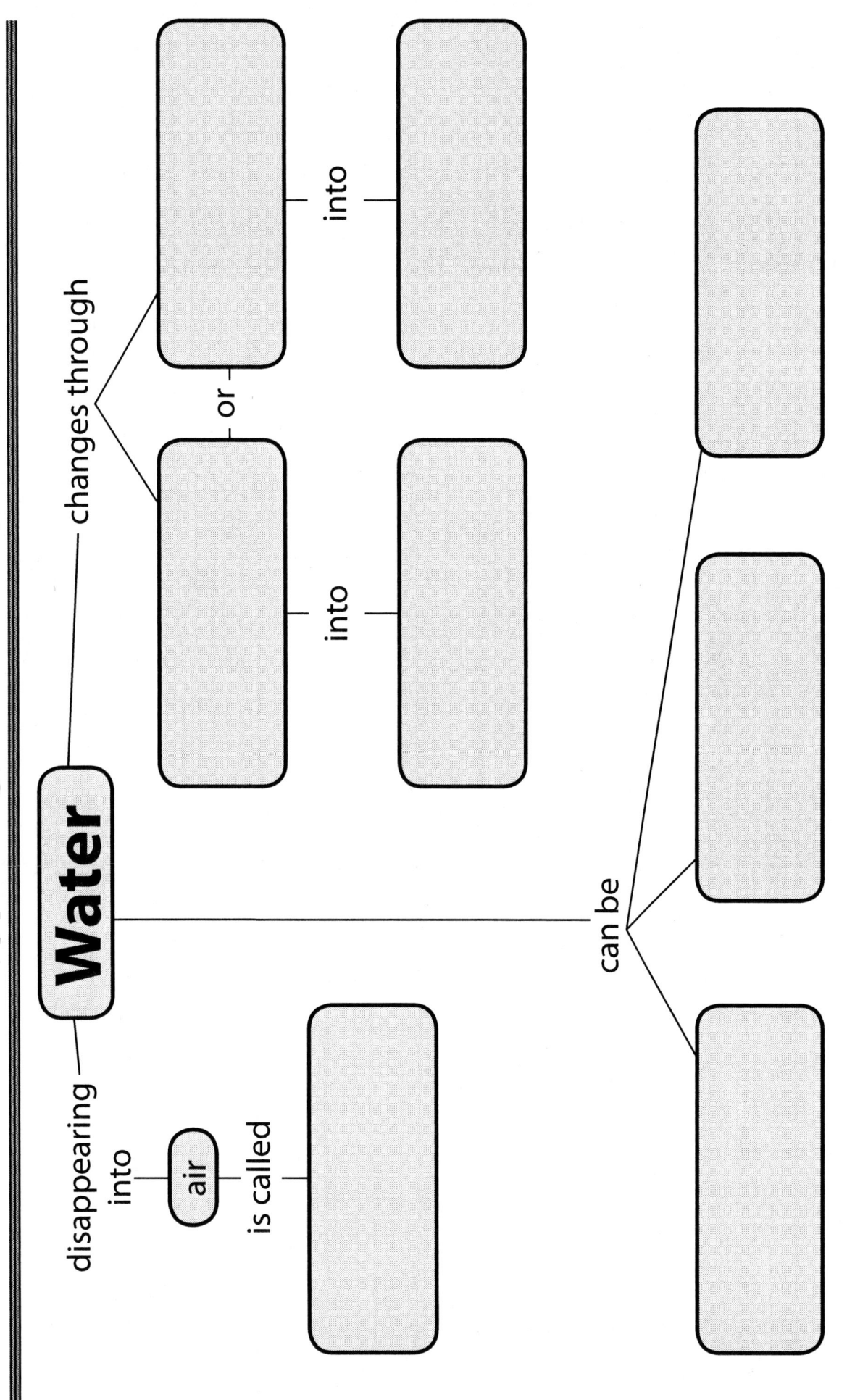

Water

- changes through ⟨ ☐ or ☐ ⟩ into ☐ / into ☐
- disappearing into (air) is called ☐
- can be ☐ / ☐ / ☐

© **Prufrock Press Inc.** • *Water Works*

This page may be photocopied or reproduced with permission for classroom use only.

Name: _____ Date: _____

Disappearing Water Concept Map
Word Bank

can be	solid	manmade	rocky	gas	sun	liquid
is called	flowing	mixing	evaporation	testing	magic	soaking
changes through	through	flowing	heating	separating	cooling	mixing
into	color	gas	liquid	pebbles	solid	rock

Lesson 7:
Can Water Reappear?

Planning the Lesson

Instructional Purposes: To use the steps in the experimentation process to study condensation; to reinforce generalizations around change; to deepen understanding of the water cycle.

Instructional Time: 45 minutes

Essential Science Understandings:
- Water can take various forms, but it is still water.
- Water can reappear in the form of condensation.
- Condensation occurs when the temperature cools, changing water vapor into liquid.

Scientific Investigation Skills and Processes:
- Make observations.
- Make predictions.
- Create a record of an experiment.
- Make inferences and draw conclusions.

Change Concept Generalizations:
- Change is everywhere.
- Change can be natural or manmade.
- Change may be perceived as orderly or random.

What to Look for in Assessment:
- Can students make a prediction?
- Can students describe what happens to water as it condenses?
- Can students record predictions and experiment steps?

Materials/Resources/Equipment:
- Student lab coats (optional)
- Small metal cans
- Markers
- Chart paper
- Plastic wrap
- Ice
- Student lab logs
- The Wheel of Scientific Investigation and Reasoning poster on p. 22

Implementing the Lesson

1. Put on lab coats and remind students that today they will try to think like scientists do. Remind students about the experiment they conducted to explain evaporation. Ask students the following questions:

a. What is evaporation?
b. Where does the water go when it evaporates or "disappears"?
c. What causes evaporation?
d. Does water evaporate when it is freezing?
e. Does water evaporate more quickly in the summer sun? Why?
f. What were the steps in our evaporation experiment?

2. Tell students that today they will investigate the opposite process. They will not observe water disappearing, but rather they will see water reappear! Although this might seem like magic, it is really a scientific process.
3. Divide the class into small groups and provide each group with an empty metal can, a piece of plastic wrap to form a lid, and some ice. Remind students that in the last experiment, they used the liquid form of water and allowed it to evaporate in the warm air. Today they will use the solid form of water (ice) to make the air cold around a metal can. Tell them not to think about the ice but to think about the cold can.
4. Complete a class chart of the steps in the experiment (the experiment section will be filled in as the students conduct the experiment):
    a. Question: Can water reappear from the air?
    b. Observations and information we know (elicit from students):
        i. Water takes different forms (solid, liquid, gas).
        ii. When we heat water, it becomes a gas.
        iii. When water is left out in the warm air, it disappears, or evaporates.

    c. Hypothesis: We think that water can reappear from the air (or we don't think water can reappear from the air).
    d. Experiment
        i. Materials:
        ii. Steps:
        iii. Data collection:
        iv. Findings:
        v. Conclusions:

5. Tell students to place several ice cubes into the can. These ice cubes will help to make the air around the can very cold.
6. Ask them to observe the outside of the can for a while, recording what is happening in their lab logs. When all cans are starting to form drops of water, ask students to think with you.
    a. What is happening?
    b. Where is the water coming from?
    c. What do we know about the water cycle?

7. Allow cans to sit for about 20 minutes while students draw pictures of the water cycle. Then, ask students to record their findings from the experiment into their lab logs. Ask students what they found out. What are their conclusions? If students have difficulty explaining what is happening, ask them to think about it. There is ice inside, but is the water from the ice now on the outside? (No). Where is the water from the ice melting? (Inside the can). Allow students to verify this. Where is the water coming from? (The water in the air, water vapor, changes into liquid water when the temperature cools. This is called *condensation*. The ice causes the vapor to turn back to water and to collect on the can. This is very noticeable when you pour a very cold drink into a warm glass. Ask students if they have ever felt

water on the outside of the glass, even when their cold drink was milk or some other liquid. This is condensation.)
8. Ask students to draw the results of their experiment as a record of their data. Review The Wheel of Scientific Investigation and Reasoning with the students, reinforcing each step as they completed it during their investigations on condensation and evaporation. Ask students to work in their small groups to decide on a few sentences they will share with the whole class to explain what they did and what they know. Allow each group to share.
9. Reread some of the pages from the two books, *A Drop of Water* and *A Drop of Water: A Book of Science and Wonder,* to focus on condensation.
10. Concluding Questions/Activities:
    a. What is the difference between evaporation and condensation?
    b. What is one thing you know about water?
    c. How does water change?
    d. How does heat affect water?
    e. How does cooling affect water?
    f. Where does the water come from when it beads up on a glass?
    g. What kinds of changes are happening during the water cycle? Are they natural or manmade?

Extending the Lesson

- Create a class mural to explain the water cycle.
- Invite small groups of students to demonstrate one of their experiments for an interested audience (e.g., principal, librarian, another small group from a different class).
- Add several books about water to the class water center. Ask students to share something they read about during class sharing time.

What to Do at Home
- Invite students to explain evaporation and condensation with their families, and to conduct the experiments again at home.

Lesson 8:
What Happens When Water Is Mixed With Other Liquids?

Planning the Lesson

Instructional Purposes: To recognize water as a solvent; to reinforce generalizations around change; to introduce the concept of density; to use data tables.

Instructional Time: 45 minutes

Essential Science Understandings:
- Some liquids will separate when mixed with water. Others will not.
- Some substances will dissolve in water. Others will not.
- Some substances will dissolve more readily in hot water than in cold water.
- Density is the relationship between an object's mass and the space it takes up.

Scientific Investigation Skills and Processes:
- Make observations.
- Apply prior knowledge to develop scientific explanations.
- Make inferences and draw conclusions.

Change Concept Generalizations:
- Change is everywhere.
- Change can be natural or manmade.
- Change may be perceived as orderly or random.

What to Look for in Assessment:
- Can students observe and record observations accurately and in detail?
- Can students describe what happens when water is mixed with other substances?
- Can students explain why some substances separate when mixed with water?
- Can students explain why some substances dissolve more readily than others?
- Can students use prior knowledge to develop scientific explanations?

Materials/Resources/Equipment:
- Student lab coats (optional)
- Clear, empty, and clean soda bottles with caps
- Markers
- Sponge
- Student lab logs
- Chart paper
- Food coloring
- Cooking oil
- Water
- Salt
- Sugar
- Balance
- Five clear plastic cups per group

- One zipper bag each of JELL-O, salt, oatmeal, baking soda, and Kool-Aid per group
- Copies of Dissolve or Not? Handout (p. 53)
- The Wheel of Scientific Investigation and Reasoning poster on p. 22

Implementing the Lesson

1. Put on lab coats and remind students that today they will think and act like scientists do. Display The Wheel of Scientific Investigation and Reasoning and ask students which part of the wheel they like the best and why. Elicit responses that discuss all sections of the wheel. Remind students that sometimes scientists don't complete every section of the wheel or do them in a particular order. Their scientific thinking guides them to sometimes skip over or come back to a particular activity. One thought may lead them down a new path.
2. Ask students to share some of the things they remember about how water changes. Ask students if they added things to water, would that make the water change? Encourage students to share something they would/could add to water to make it change. Would the water look the same? Can they think of something that they could add to water and make it look the same?
3. Put students in groups of 3–4, give each group five clear plastic cups with water, a spoon, and zipper bags of JELL-O, oatmeal, baking soda, Kool-Aid, and salt. Explain to students that some things dissolve in water and some do not.
4. Post the definition of dissolve: to mix with a liquid so that the result is a liquid that is the same throughout.
5. Tell students that they will continue to think and act like scientists. Distribute copies of the Dissolve or Not? handout to students (see p. 53). Explain that students need to look at each substance and make a prediction or hypothesis about whether they think it will dissolve or not. They should circle the Yes in the Hypothesis column if they think it will dissolve or No if they do not think it will dissolve. Then, after they try to dissolve the substances in the water, they should circle Yes or No.
6. Once students have completed this activity, engage them in a discussion using the following questions as a guide.
    a. How did the water change as you added the products?
    b. What generalization of change does this fit?
7. Demonstrate how a scale can hold water, using a sponge.
    a. Show students a sponge. Ask them, "What happens when water is poured onto a sponge?"
    b. Place one sponge in a clear container. Pour a small amount of water on the sponge. What happened to the water?
8. Continue pouring water onto the sponge. Discuss observations. Once the sponge is full of water or saturated, it can hold no more liquid. Ask students to hold the liquid and then the dry sponge and answer, "How are their weights different?"
9. Explain that water can hold some solids like a sponge can hold water. This is called *dissolving*.
10. Add a few drops of food coloring to a cup of water. Ask students if the color dissolved in the water. Now add a teaspoon of salt to the water and have a student stir the solution.
11. Have students describe what they observe. Explain that when the salt dissolved, it broke apart into smaller pieces and is held in the water like the water was held in the sponge.

12. Model dissolving by having four students stand shoulder to shoulder. Place objects like balls between their shoulders so they are held in place by the pressure. Explain that the small particles of salt are held in the water rather than settling to the bottom.
13. Ask them to think of something else that will dissolve in water. List their responses on chart paper. Tell students that they will be able to test some of these in the water center later.
14. Next, show the students containers of water and oil. Explain to the students that everything will not dissolve in water. Provide each student with a few drops of oil and ask them to rub their hands together to coat their hands with the oil. Invite students to put their hands (one at a time) into the container of water at their table. Have students describe what happened to the water and the oil.
15. Tell students that you are going to put some water into the bottle and then add some oil. Based on their experience with the oil on their hands, what do they predict will happen? Put the water into the bottle, about ⅓ full. Tell students you are adding a couple of drops of food coloring so that they can see the water better. Next, invite a student to help you put about the same amount of oil into the bottle. Ask students to describe what happens. Shake the bottle gently and again ask students to describe what happens.
16. Allow students to work with a partner to replicate the experiment. Put the oil into the bottles ahead of time and allow students to mix the water and coloring and then pour it into the bottle. Ask students to record and draw pictures in their lab logs to remember what they observed. Be sure students tighten the cap on the bottle securely before gently moving the liquids!
17. Ask students to describe what happens when they move the liquids in the bottle. Do they mix together? Do they stay mixed after several minutes? Remind students to enter data into their lab logs.
18. When all students have finished, ask them to think about the two liquids in the bottle. How might they be different? Measure out about ½ cup of oil into one container and ½ cup of water into another. Using a balance, measure the mass of the liquids in each cup and record the masses onto a chart. Ask students which one has a greater mass. Think back to our experiment mixing oil and water. As time passed, which substance floated to the top? Why?
19. Explain to students that the oil stays on top because it is less dense than water. If you have the same amount of two different substances (oil and water), and one has less mass than the other (oil weighs less than water), then the substance with less mass is less dense and will float on the top (oil floats on top). Remind students that you put the same amount of oil and water into the bottle (same volume). Because they did not mix together, they must have different masses, although they look like the same amount. If two objects take up the same amount of space (volume), and object A has a greater mass than object B, then A is denser than B.
20. Let students know that they will learn more about density in the next few lessons.
21. Concluding Questions/Activities:
    a. Explain what *dissolve* means.
    b. What are some things that dissolve in water?
    c. What is density?
    d. What happens when one substance is denser than the other and they are put together?
    e. What happened to the oil and water? Why?
    f. What is one thing a scientist does to investigate things?
    g. What are some examples of change with water?

Extending the Lesson

- Place tightly-sealed bottles with one cup of each of the following liquids: water, colored water, shampoo, oil, vinegar, and lotion at the water center. Record the mass of each cup of liquid and place labels on each bottle with the name of the liquid, its mass, and an identifying letter (e.g., A, B, C). Invite students to compare two of the bottles for density. Which one is denser? What does that mean?
- Caution students never to mix liquids without adult supervision. Some liquids should never be mixed together because they might form a chemical reaction that could cause them harm. Demonstrate this fact by mixing vinegar with baking soda to show that they react with each other in a chemical way that might be dangerous. In this case they are not.
- Add several books to the water center that focus on density, sinking, and floating, in anticipation of the next lessons.

What to Do at Home

- Ask students to find pictures of things that are heavy for their size (dense) or quite light for their size. Create a class chart of things that are dense and things that are not dense.

Name: _____ Date: _____

Dissolve or Not?

	Hypothesis	**Dissolve or Not**
Baking Soda	Yes or No	Yes or No
JELL-O	Yes or No	Yes or No
Kool-Aid	Yes or No	Yes or No
Oatmeal	Yes or No	Yes or No
Salt	Yes or No	Yes or No

Lesson 9: What Is Density?

Planning the Lesson

Instructional Purpose: To engage students in sorting objects based on size and density and comparing the relative density of two objects.

Instructional Time: 45 minutes

Essential Science Understandings:
- Our senses help us to seek, find, and react to information.
- Certain objects float in water while others do not float.

Scientific Investigation Skills and Processes:
- Make observations.
- Ask questions.
- Learn more.
- Create meaning.

Change Concept Generalizations:
- Change is everywhere.
- Change may be random or predictable.

What to Look for in Assessment:
- Students can quickly and comfortably describe a range of characteristics with a variety of words.
- Students can describe what density means.

Materials/Resources/Equipment:
- A set of at least 12 objects for each group of 3–4 students (e.g., toy cars, clay, soft balls, stuffed animals, erasers, feathers, rocks, leaves, shells, acorns, buttons, checkers)
- Four sections of sentence strips, each labeled with a physical property: Color, Shape, Texture/Feel, Size/Mass
- Student lab coats (optional)
- A piece of red and blue construction paper for each group
- Density blocks
- Small clear plastic containers such as baby food containers
- Pennies
- Balance
- Copies of Comparing My Toys handout on p. 57
- Chart paper
- Markers
- The Wheel of Scientific Investigation and Reasoning poster on p. 22

Implementing the Lesson

1. Ask students to put on their lab coats.
2. Tell students that they are going to learn to see some everyday things in a new way. This is a skill that scientists use, so it will help us learn to think like scientists.
3. Present the various items you have selected for this experiment.
    a. Refer to The Wheel of Scientific Investigation and Reasoning Ask Questions section.
    b. Ask the following questions:
        i. How are these items different?
        ii. Are any of them similar?
        iii. In what way(s) are they similar or different?

4. Ask students to notice the section on The Wheel of Scientific Investigation and Reasoning called Learn More.
5. Remind students that one way scientists learn more is by observing. Define *observe* as *to carefully watch someone or something* (Scholastic, 1996).
6. Ask students: How is *observing* different from just *looking* at something?
7. Name something that you need to observe. Name something you just look at instead.
8. Divide the class into groups of 3–4 students. Give each group a piece of the red and blue paper and a set of objects to sort.
9. Tell students that they are going to classify the objects into two different groups.
10. Explain that scientists make observations about specific categories. Display the sentence strip with the word "Shape." Ask which senses would be appropriate for observing shape.
11. Have students divide their objects into two groups in any way they can based on shape. Students can decide on the two groups themselves.
12. Place one group of objects on the red paper and one on the blue paper to keep the groups separate. After a few minutes, have each group of students share how they classified their objects. Repeat classifying and questioning for each category:
    a. Shape
    b. Color
    c. Texture/Feel
    d. Size/Mass

13. Ask students if they have any objects that are about the same size but have a different mass. Have them describe the differences they have observed. This is called *density*, which is *how light or heavy something is for its size* (Scholastic, 1996).
14. If two objects take up the same amount of space but have different masses, they have different densities.
15. Pass around density blocks and have students observe the differences. Which is the lightest cube? The heaviest? Have a volunteer arrange all blocks in order from least dense to most dense. If these blocks are not available, use several small boxes of the same size filled with different amounts of washers or pennies hidden inside.
16. Place students back into groups of 3–4 students. Give each group a clear plastic container (small, plastic baby food containers work well) and a stack of pennies.
17. Have students place five pennies into the container and ask:
    a. Has the size of the container changed?
    b. Has the mass changed?
    c. What can you say about the density?

18. Each time pennies are added to the container, the teacher should measure the mass of the container and record the mass on a class chart.
19. Continue adding pennies and ask questions until they are clear on the concept that if the size remains the same but the mass changes, the density is changing. Ask students the following questions:
    a. Is this a natural or a manmade change?
    b. Can we predict what will happen with more pennies?

20. Review the concept of density by having students imagine they are holding a box full of feathers.
    a. How does the box feel?
    b. Now imagine that it suddenly feels a little heavier. Act out the change.
    c. What has changed? (It is denser.) What could be inside?
    d. The box is even heavier now. You can barely hold it up because it is so dense. What could be inside?
    e. The box is so heavy you can't even pick it up. What extremely dense substance could be filling your box now?

21. Ask the students to repeat the word that explains how light or heavy something is for its size (density).
22. Concluding Questions and/or Actions:
    a. Are larger objects always heavier? Think of an example to prove your answer.
    b. How is making observations like a scientist different from how you usually look at objects?

Extending the Lesson

What to Do at Home

- Give students the Comparing My Toys handout on p. 57 to take home. Ask students to choose two of their favorite toys and compare their size, shape, color, and texture. How are they alike? How are they different? Parents are encouraged to work with the students to help record their answers.

Name:_____   Date:_____

Comparing My Toys

Dear Parents,

We are describing objects at school in terms of size, color, shape, and texture. Ask your child to select two favorite toys and describe each of them in terms of these four characteristics. Please record what your child says for each toy in the spaces below. Then ask, "How are your toys alike? How are they different?" This activity provides excellent practice in learning to look carefully at objects, an important skill in science.

	Toy #1 _____	Toy # _____
Size		
Shape		
Color		
Texture		

© Prufrock Press Inc. • *Water Works*
This page may be photocopied or reproduced with permission for classroom use only.

Lesson 10:
Which Things Sink and Float?

Planning the Lesson

Instructional Purpose: To engage students in an exploration of the concept of density and in predicting which things will sink and which will float.

Instructional Time: 45 minutes

Essential Science Understandings:
- Water can be a solid, liquid, or gas.
- Certain objects float in water while others do not float.

Scientific Investigation Skills and Processes:
- Design and conduct the experiment.

Change Concept Generalizations:
- Change can be natural or manmade.
- Change can be orderly or random.

What to Look for in Assessment:
- Can students explain the concept of density?
- Can students make a prediction (sink or float) and explain their reason?
- Can students give accurate predictions about sinking and floating?
- Can students state a hypothesis about whether an object would sink or float?

Materials/Resources/Equipment:
- Clear plastic containers with greater width than depth, one per group
- A large container of water to use in demonstration and to fill students' containers
- Labels "Sink" and "Float" for each table group
- One spoon per group
- Copies of Sink or Float? data table (p. 61)
- Student lab coats (optional)
- Items to test: crayons, pencils, plastic classroom toys, wood blocks, paperclips, rocks, leaves, shells, acorns, feathers, coins, checkers, buttons (these items will be placed in water)
- Density blocks
- Masking tape
- The Wheel of Scientific Investigation and Reasoning poster (p. 22)
- Students' lab logs

Implementing the Lesson

1. Have students put on their lab coats and explain that as scientists, they are going to be studying some of the properties of water.
2. Reinforce the concept of density. Use masking tape to create a square on the floor large enough for the entire class to stand in if they are close together.
3. Hold up the lightest density block and have one student stand in the square. Discuss how the square and the student represent the density of the block.
4. Hold up the next density block. Ask how the number of students needs to change to increase the density. Have two students stand in the square.
5. Continue changing blocks and adding students. Point out that the size of the square never changes but as more students are added, it will have more mass and the students will be closer together.
6. Refer to The Wheel of Scientific Investigation and Reasoning Ask Questions section. On a chart, place the question, "Will it sink or float?" and explain that this is their scientific question for today.
7. Next, refer to the wheel's Design and Conduct the Experiment section. (*Note:* You will need to discuss forming a hypothesis with the students.) Review that a prediction is *a good guess about what will happen*. A scientist's prediction is a hypothesis about an experiment. Before beginning an experiment, you need a prediction about whether the object will sink or float.
8. Demonstrate the process using progressively heavier density blocks. Ask the class to make a prediction for each, then test it. Record the data on a chart such as the one in Table 5.

Table 5
Sink or Float Chart

Density Block	Does It Sink or Float?
Block #1	
Block #2	
Block #3	
Block #4	

9. Next, have one child demonstrate the experiment, using one of the objects.
10. Point out the current water level as marked by the line.
11. Have the child pick up an object (other than a coin or checker) and make a prediction ("I think it will sink/float.").
12. Ask students, "What do you already know about sinking and floating that helps you make a prediction?"
13. Test the object. Ask the students the following:
    a. Was your prediction accurate?
    b. What did you notice about the water level? Was there a change?

14. Demonstrate the process a second time with a coin or checker.
15. Place students in small groups of 3–4.
16. Each child will choose one item to test.

17. Allow about 5 minutes to test the items.
18. Have students remove the objects and place them on the paper towel in front of the correct word label: Sink or Float.
19. On the Sink or Float? chart (see p. 61), have students draw a picture of selected items and record an "S" for sink and an "F" for float.
20. Ask students to describe what is similar about everything that floated.
    a. Discuss mass and shape.
    b. What was the same about the things that sank?
    c. What two objects were similar in size but had different densities?
    d. Did most dense objects usually sink?
    e. How did the water level change?

21. Concluding Question/Activities:
    a. What did we learn in this lesson?
    b. What is similar about everything that floated? What was the same about the things that sank?
    c. Name a very small object that would sink and a very large object that would float.
    d. Do you think that objects will sink or float the same way in all liquids?
    e. How did the water level change?

Extending the Lesson

Journal Questions and/or Prompts
(have students record their responses in the lab logs)
- Draw a picture of something floating.
- Write a sentence about it.

Technology Connection
- The "Sorting and Using Materials" game found at the following Web site would be good for advanced students. It allows them to test household objects to see of they are waterproof and/or bendy then sort and classify the products in a grid. See http://www.bbc.co.uk/schools/scienceclips/ages/5_6/sorting_using_mate.shtml
- For students who are reading, the grouping game at the same Web site would offer additional challenge. See http://www.bbc.co.uk/schools/scienceclips/ages/6_7/grouping_materials.shtml

What to Do at Home
- Find a picture of something that is floating or that has sunk. How did it get there? Was it manmade or natural?

Name:_____ Date:_____

Sink or Float?

Item	Sink or Float?

Lesson 11: Can We Make a Better Floater?

Planning the Lesson

Instructional Purpose: To guide students in learning about displacement and design of clay boats to hold more weight.

Instructional Time: 45 minutes

Essential Science Understandings:
- Water can be a solid, liquid, or gas.
- Certain objects float in water while others do not float.

Scientific Investigation Skills and Processes:
- Design and conduct the experiment.

Change Concept Generalization:
- Change can be examined orderly or random.

What to Look for in Assessment:
- Can students count and record the number of weights each shape could support?
- Cam students relate the change in shape to the change in the weight supported?

Materials/Resources/Equipment:
- *Who Sank the Boat?* by P. Allen, published by Coward-McCann
- Clear plastic containers wider than they are deep, one per group and one for demonstration (disposable containers work well)
- Plastic toy boat, one per group
- Modeling clay, a small lump for each child
- Weights—pennies, washers, or other small objects
- Student lab coats (optional)
- Markers
- Copies of Objects in Water Concept Map (p. 65)
- Copies/Transparency of Floating Boats Data Table (p. 67)
- Chart paper
- The Wheel of Scientific Investigation and Reasoning poster (p. 22)

Implementing the Lesson

1. Tell students: "We are going to create a new concept map about objects in water." Show students a transparency of the Objects in Water Concept Map (p. 65) or distribute copies of the page for student use. Use the following questions to guide the students in completing the concept map.
    a. What have we learned about objects in water?
    b. What are some examples of objects that float? Sink?

c. What have we learned about objects dissolving in water?
   d. What are some examples of objects that dissolve?

> **Teacher's Note:** Have a plastic container half full of water and a collection of items to test at each station. With a permanent marker, draw a line on the outside of the container at the water level.

2. Use the Sample Water Concept Map on p. 66 as a guide during completion of the concept map.
3. Have students put on their lab coats and remind students that during the lesson, they will think like scientists do.
4. Read aloud *Who Sank the Boat?* by Pamela Allen. Ask students how this story relates to their last experiment.
5. Refer to The Wheel of Scientific Investigation and Reasoning Ask Questions section. Ask students, "Do you have any questions we could ask about floating clay because of the story?"
6. Move to the next space on the wheel: Learn More.
7. Explain that water pushes up on anything that is placed in water.
8. Show students a lump of clay and a clear plastic container with water. Would the clay sink or float in water?
9. Have a student demonstrate that it will sink by dropping the clay in the water.
10. Point out the water level. Did the water level change? What made the change occur?
11. Define *displacement* as *to take the place of something else*. Ask the students
    a. What took the place of some of the water?
    b. Where did the water go?

12. Place the test items in the water one at a time. Instruct students to watch the water level and how it changes as different amounts of water are displaced by the objects. Ask the following questions:
    a. What object displaced (moved) the most water? The least water?
    b. What makes a difference in how much water was displaced?

13. Divide students into groups of 3–4. Provide each group with a container of water.
14. Give each student a lump of clay. Have each student make changes to the shape of their clay so that it will float. Ask the students:
    a. How can you change the clay to make it float?
    b. Is this change random (no reason or pattern) or is it orderly (is there a reason for the change)?

15. Have several students explain the reason that they changed the clay into the shape that they chose.
16. Have students continue to attempt to create and test their new clay shapes. If they need assistance, show them a toy boat and talk about why the boat floats and how they could copy the shape. Remind students that they will make a good guess about what will happen. Help students phrase the hypothesis in statements such as "The flat clay will hold the most weight" or "The bowl shaped clay will float better." Write the hypothesis on the board or chart paper. Ask students, "When the clay is rolled up into a ball, how much space does the water have to push against?" (All of the weight is concentrated in that one spot.)
17. Now flatten out the clay. Tell the children to look at how much space the water has to push against now. This shape helps the clay float. By making the bottom of a boat into a shape that has lots of space for the water to push against, even metal floats.
18. Refer to the next space on The Wheel of Scientific Investigation and Reasoning: Design and Conduct the Experiment. Students are going to investigate how much

weight different floating shapes can support. Have students form their clay into a flat circle.
19. On the chart paper, create a chart with the two sides labeled "Circle" and "Bowl."
20. Model floating the piece of clay to check for the effect of adding weight. Add weights while counting them until the clay sinks. Write the number on the appropriate place on the chart. Demonstrate forming the clay into more of a bowl shape, with edges that angle up like a boat.
21. Have students create a hypothesis about the two shapes: Which one do they think will hold the most weight?
22. Direct students to the next space on The Wheel of Scientific Investigation and Reasoning: Create Meaning. Place student in groups of 3–4. Give each a copy of the Floating Boats Data Table on p. 67. Each group member should write their name in a space under the word name.
23. Have them test each shape, working together to count the number of weights the clay will support. Assist students in reforming the clay to test the second shape. When they have finished and compared the two shapes, allow students to create and test their own shape.
24. After the experiments are complete, bring students together to discuss the results. Copy the number of weights held onto a large data table on chart paper. Circle the largest number a boat held for each child in red to indicate the boat that held the most. As they look at all the red circled numbers, ask them if they can tell which shape held the most weight.
25. Ask students: What did the experiment show? Was the hypothesis true or false? Pass around a toy boat. Do your results fit with the shape of a boat? How?
26. Direct students to the next space on the wheel: Tell Others What Was Found.
27. One way to share information from an experiment is to graph it.
28. Graph the results using a human graph.
29. Have students line up to indicate if their flat boat, bowl-shaped boat, or their own design held the most weight.
30. Concluding Questions/Activities:
    a. How did changing the shape change how much weight the clay could hold?
    b. Does changing the shape change the density?
    c. Did you use the information from your experiment when you made your own shape?
    d. Did the results from the class experiment match the boat designs that you observed?
    e. Were the changes in the amount of weight the boat could hold similar? Is the change orderly or random?

Extending the Lesson

- If Internet access is available or if you are using books from the library, look at several boat designs and compare the designs to the toy boat and the clay boats.
    - http://www.boatdesign.net/gallery/showphoto.php/photo/1196/cat/512
    - http://www.fish.state.pa.us/angleroater/1999/julaug99/boathull.htm

What to Do at Home
- At home or in the classroom, find objects that have a rounded shape similar to the bottom of a boat. Do you think they would float?

Name: _____   Date: _____

Objects in Water Concept Map

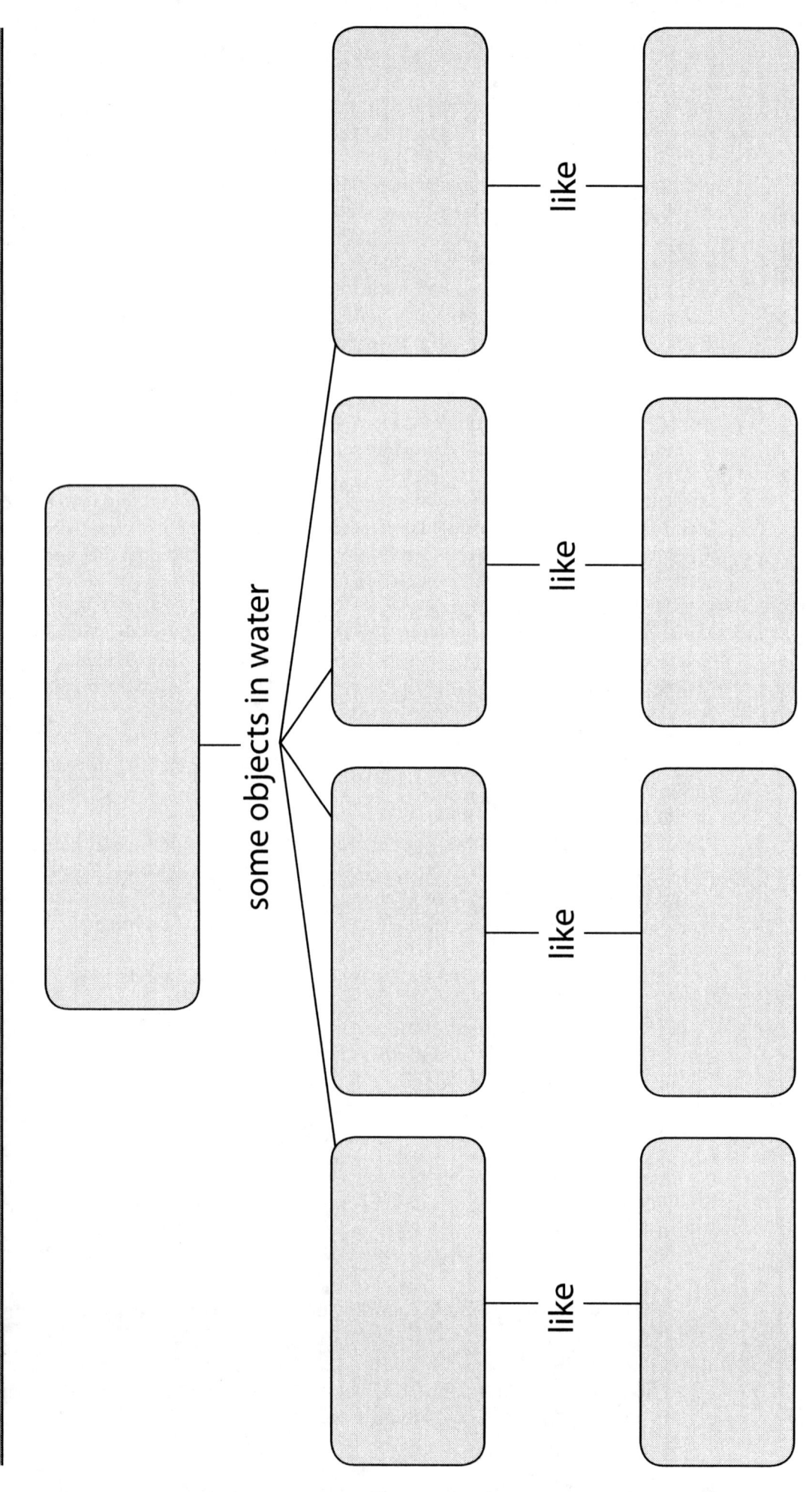

some objects in water

like

like

like

like

Name: _____ Date: _____

Sample Water Concept Map

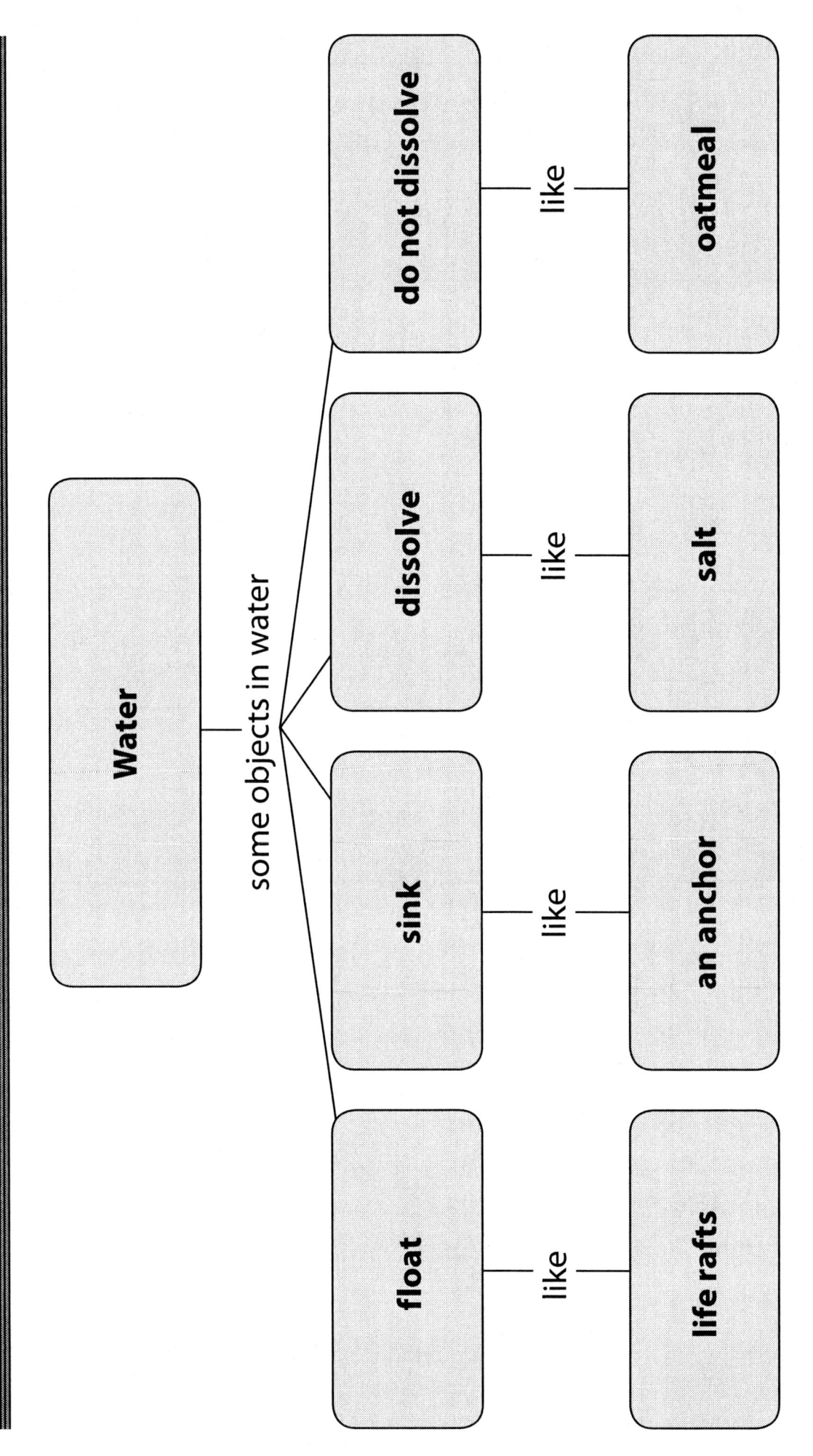

```
                          Water
                            |
                   some objects in water
          ┌─────────┬───────┴───────┬──────────┐
        float      sink          dissolve    do not dissolve
          |         |                |              |
         like      like             like           like
          |         |                |              |
      life rafts  an anchor         salt         oatmeal
```

Name:_____ Date:_____

Floating Boats Data Table

How many weights did your clay boat hold? Write the number in the box.

Name	Number of Weights
Flat Boat	
Bowl-Shaped Boat	
My Own Shape	

Lesson 12:
What Have We Learned About Water?

Planning the Lesson

Instructional Purpose: To engage students in a review of what they have learned, giving examples of something they did in class that matches change generalizations, scientific processes, and essential content learning.

Instructional Time: Allow 15 minutes per center. You may choose to complete centers over several days.

Essential Science Understandings:
- Water can be a solid, liquid, or gas.
- The state of water changes by heating or cooling.
- Water evaporates into the air.
- Water condenses on cold surfaces.
- Some liquids will separate when mixed with water.
- Some substances will dissolve in water while others will not.
- Certain objects float in water while others do not float.
- Some solids dissolve in water and others do not.

Science Investigation Skills and Processes:
- Create meaning.
- Tell others what was found.

Change Concept Generalizations:
- Change is everywhere.
- Change can be natural or manmade.
- Change can be perceived as orderly or random.
- Change relates to time.

What to Look for in Assessment:
- Can students develop scientific questions about water?
- Can students identify examples of changes to water and relate them to change generalizations?
- Can students give examples of condensation and evaporation?
- Can students predict which liquids are more or less dense than water?
- Can students figure out how to make an object float?
- Can students describe the concept of density?

Teacher's Note: The materials for the six centers should be prepared ahead of time. Volunteers will be needed to help run each center. Students should be divided into small groups with a card that designates when they go to each center.

Implementing the Lesson

1. Have students put on lab coats.
2. Explain to the students that they will rotate through six centers to review what they have been learning about water. Information about each center is included on pp. 70–71.
3. Allow the students to rotate through the centers.
4. Concluding Questions/Activities: Conduct a final discussion with the students after all centers have been completed.
    a. What was your favorite center? Why?
    b. What do you think is another important question you could ask about water?
    c. What can you tell about the parts of The Wheel of Scientific Investigation and Reasoning?
    d. Change is everywhere! Do you remember some examples of noticing change all around you?
    e. What does it mean if a change is natural? Can you give an example?
    f. What is something about water that takes time to change?
    g. How do scientists know something has changed?
    h. Can you tell when something is going to change?

Extending the Lesson

- Provide a center activity with a list of linking words and picture cards. Use either general pictures or pictures specific to the unit. Encourage students to practice making mapping sentences by using two cards and connecting them with linking words.

Lesson 12 Centers

Center 1: What do scientists want to know? Make up a scientific question.

Materials/Resources/Equipment
- Cup of water
- Salt
- Oil
- Block of wood
- Cards depicting various images of water
- Lump of clay
- Small rocks
- Ice cubes
- Hard-boiled egg
- Pencils
- Paper

These materials should be placed on the table. Students are instructed to examine the items and think about what a scientist could ask or want to know about these objects. The students can respond by writing down their answer, drawing it, or saying it to the volunteer at the center.

Center 2: What can we say about water and change?

Materials/Resources/Equipment
- Collection of miscellaneous pictures, some of which represent change generalizations
- Copies of Change Generalizations handout (p. 72)
- Pencils

Students use the generalizations about change and try to find one or more pictures that depict the generalization. For example, a student might match a picture of a swimming pool with the generalization "Change can be natural or manmade." If sufficient pictures are available, students may glue one picture onto their worksheet for each generalization. Alternatively, they may draw pictures. If volunteers are available at the tables, students should explain their selections.

Center 3 and 4: Will it dissolve?

Materials/Resources/Equipment
- Cups
- Pitcher of hot water
- Pitcher of cold water
- Packets of sugar
- Packets of salt
- Pencils and paper

Center 3

Ask students to think like a scientist and design an experiment about things dissolving in water. What is their research question? Tell students to work with a partner to write down a question, the materials they would use, and the steps they would take in their experiment.

Center 4

Ask partners to work together and conduct the experiment. They are to record their data and tell what they found.

Note: These two parts do not have to be done one after the other. Students need to bring their work from Part I to complete Part II.

Center 5: Can it float?

Materials/Resources/Equipment
- Two pieces of aluminum foil (per student)
- Container of water for floating foil boats with pennies
- 4–5 pennies

Students are to shape one piece of aluminum foil with the 4–5 pennies so that it sinks. Students are to shape a second piece of aluminum foil with the 4–5 pennies so that it floats. Students are then asked, "Why did you choose these shapes?" They should draw the shapes of their boats and label them as "sink" or "float."

Center 6: Where is the water?

Materials/Resources/Equipment
- One glass per two students
- Ice
- Plastic wrap
- Paper and pencil
- Saucers per two students

Ask students to use the materials at this center to demonstrate condensation or evaporation. Students should select one or the other and then tell the steps they would take to complete their experiment. Steps may be recorded in pictures and/or words. For students who may have difficulty, a set of picture cards may be developed to show the possible steps. The student would select and order the steps for either of the experiments.

Name:_____ Date:_____

Change Generalizations
What Do We Know About Change?

1. Change is everywhere.

2. Change is related to time.

3. Change can be natural or manmade.

4. Change may be random or orderly.

Appendices

Appendix A: Science Safety

Instructional Purpose: To instill in students the importance of safety in the classroom; to outline science safety rules to be implemented throughout the unit.

Instructional Time: 45 minutes

Materials/Resources/Equipment:
- Plastic disposable gloves
- Safety goggles
- Chart paper
- Markers
- Science Safety Guidelines (see p. 76)
- Science Safety Rules printed on chart paper (see p. 77)
- Sample materials:
  - Plant
  - Plastic bag of nonhazardous powdery substance (e.g., sugar)
  - Closed jar of nonhazardous liquid (e.g., water)
  - Lit candle
  - Sharp object or replica of a sharp object

Activities

1. Display sample materials on a long table in front of students. Inform students that they will soon begin a science unit in which they will observe and study many different kinds of materials, such as these. Explain that it is important for students to practice safety during the investigations. Relate the necessity of science safety rules with those of the classroom and physical education.
2. Display and define each item. Tell students that as a class they will create a list of rules they should follow when handling these materials. Have students think of how they can keep their bodies safe. Record these on chart paper.
3. Next, unveil the Science Safety Rules (p. 77) on chart paper. Have students compare the two lists. How do students' examples relate to these rules? If necessary, add additional rules to the list.
4. Explain why some materials (such as knives) or elements (such as fire) are never appropriate for children to handle in school. Briefly discuss the potential hazards associated with these. *Note:* Please read the Science Safety Guidelines on p. 76 prior to teaching this lesson.
5. Finally, conduct a brief demonstration to illustrate how to practice safety guidelines. Take the plastic bag containing a nonhazardous powdery substance and the jar of nonhazardous liquid. Explain that you are going to investigate how the two materials interact. Ask students how you can be safe while doing this investigation. Reinforce that substances can be harmful to the eyes or skin and that they should *never* be ingested. Explain that the same is true of plants, which can be toxic to humans. Emphasize that students should follow similar guidelines when studying plants.
6. Following students' examples of safety measures, demonstrate how to use safety goggles to protect the eyes, plastic gloves to protect the hands, and other relevant

protective measures, such as pinning long hair back and wearing appropriate clothing. Conduct the demonstration by carefully pouring the powdery substance into the jar of liquid. Emphasize that you should never touch your face or mouth (and especially should not eat or drink) during science experiments.

7. Tell students that materials will be disposed of properly by the teacher after the investigation is completed. Students should not touch any potentially harmful substances.
8. Demonstrate the final rule (Wash your hands) by properly removing the gloves (without the outside of the gloves ever touching the body), and the goggles. If there is a sink in the classroom, demonstrate how to properly wash hands. If no sink is present, inform students that after each investigation the class will go to the bathroom to wash their hands.
9. Conclude the lesson by emphasizing that science investigations are interesting and fun, but they can also be dangerous if not conducted properly. By following the Science Safety Rules, the class will enjoy the benefits of learning about science.

Science Safety Guidelines

1. Know and follow your school's policies and procedures regarding classroom safety.

2. Always provide direct adult supervision when students are engaging in scientific experimentation.

3. Ensure that all materials and equipment are safe for handling by primary students.

4. Exert extra caution when materials have the potential for harm when used improperly.

5. Use protective gear for eyes, skin, and breathing when conducting experiments and require students to do the same.

6. Always conduct an experiment by yourself before completing it with the students.

7. Store materials for experiments out of the reach of students.

8. Never allow students to eat or drink during science experiments.

9. Follow general safety rules for sharp objects, heated items, breakables, or spilled liquids.

10. Teach students that it is unsafe to touch their face, mouth, eyes, or other body parts when they are working with plants, animals, microorganisms, or chemicals. Wash hands prior to touching. Caution students about putting anything in their mouth or breathing in the smell of substances.

11. Be aware of students' allergies to plants including plant pollen, animals, foods, chemicals, or other substances to be used in the science classroom. Take all precautions necessary. Common food allergens include peanuts, tree nuts (cashews, almonds, walnuts, hazelnuts, macadamia nuts, pecans, pistachios, and pine nuts), shellfish, fish, milk, eggs, wheat, and soy.

12. Use caution with plants. Never allow students to pick or handle any unknown plants, leaves, flowers, seeds, or berries. Use gloves to touch unknown plants. Many common house, garden, and wooded area plants are toxic.

13. Avoid glass jars and containers. Use plastic, paper, or cloth containers.

14. Thermometers should be filled with alcohol, not mercury.

15. Clearly label any chemicals used and dispose of properly.

16. Teach students safety rules for science including:

    - **Always** do scientific experiments with an adult present.

    - **Never** mix things together (liquids, powders) without adult approval.

    - **Use** your senses carefully. Protect your eyes, ears, nose, mouth, and skin.

    - **Wash your hands** after using materials for an experiment.

Name: _____ Date: _____

Science Safety Rules

1. **Always** do scientific experiments with an adult present.

2. **Never** mix things together (liquids, powders) without adult approval.

3. **Use** your senses carefully. Protect your eyes, ears, nose, mouth, and skin.

4. **Wash your hands** after using materials for an experiment.

Appendix B: Teaching Models

Several teaching models are incorporated into the Project Clarion units. These models ensure emphasis on unit outcomes and support student understanding of the concepts and processes that are the focus of each unit. Teachers should become familiar with these models and how to use them before teaching the unit. The first three models are used in every Project Clarion unit. The last model is used as appropriate to the outcomes of the specific units. The models are listed below and outlined in the pages that follow.

1. The Taba Model of Concept Development
2. The Wheel of Scientific Investigation and Reasoning
3. Concept Mapping
4. Frayer Model of Vocabulary Development

The Taba Model of Concept Development

Each Project Clarion unit supports the development of a specific overarching concept (patterns, change, systems, or cause and effect). The concept development model, based upon the work of Hilda Taba (1962), supports student learning of the overarching concept. The model involves both inductive and deductive reasoning processes and focuses on the creation of generalizations about the overarching concept from a student-derived list of created concept examples. The model includes a series of steps, with each step involving student participation. Students begin with a broad concept, determine specific examples from that broad concept, create appropriate categorization systems, cite nonexamples of the concept, establish generalizations based on their understanding, and then apply the generalizations to their readings and other situations.

The model generally is most effective when small groups of students work through each step, with whole-class debriefing following each stage of the process. However, with primary-age students, additional teacher guidance may be necessary, especially for the later stages of the model. The steps of the model are outlined below, using the unit concept of change.

1. Students generate examples of the concept of change, derived from their own understanding and experiences with change in the world. Teachers should encourage students to provide at least 15–20 examples; a class list may be created out of the small-group lists to lengthen the set of changes students have to work with.
2. Students then group their changes into categories. This process allows students to search for interrelatedness and to organize their thinking. It often is helpful to have individual examples written on cards so that the categorization may occur physically, as well as mentally or in writing. Students then should explain their reasoning for their categorization system and seek clarification from each other as a whole group. Teachers should ensure that all examples have been accounted for in the categorization system established.
3. Students then generate a list of nonexamples of the concept of change. Teachers may begin this step with the direction, "Now list examples of things that *do not*

change." Encourage students to think carefully about their nonexamples and discuss ideas within their groups. Each group should list five to six nonexamples.
4. The students next determine generalizations about the concept of change, using their lists of examples, categories, and nonexamples. Teachers then should share the unit generalizations and relate valid student generalizations to the unit list. Both lists should be posted in the room throughout the course of the unit.
5. During the unit, students are asked to identify specific examples of the generalizations from their own readings, or to describe how the concept applies to a given situation about which they have read. Students also are asked to apply the generalizations to their own writings and their own lives. Several lessons employ a chart that lists several of the generalizations and asks students to supply examples specifically related to the reading or activity of that lesson.

The Wheel of Scientific Investigation and Reasoning

All scientists work to improve our knowledge and understanding of the world. In the process of scientific inquiry, scientists connect evidence with logical reasoning. Scientists also apply their imagination as they devise hypotheses and explanations that make sense of the evidence. Students can strengthen their understanding of particular science topics through investigations that cause them to employ evidence gathering, logical reasoning, and creativity. The Wheel of Scientific Investigation and Reasoning contains the specific processes involved in scientific inquiry to guide students' thinking and actions.

Make Observations

Scientists make careful observation and try things out. They must describe things as accurately as possible so that they can compare their observations from one time to another and so that they can compare their observations with those of other scientists. Scientists use their observations to form questions for investigation.

Ask Questions

Scientific investigations usually are initiated through a problem to be solved or a question to be asked. Selecting just the right question or clearly defining the problem to be addressed is critical to the investigation process.

Learn More

To clarify their questions, scientists learn more by reviewing bodies of scientific knowledge documented in text and in previously conducted investigations. Also, when scientists get conflicting information from the information they have gathered, they make fresh observations and insights that may result in revision of the previously formed question. By learning more, scientists can design and conduct more effective experiments or build upon previously conducted experiments.

Design and Conduct the Experiment

Scientists use their collection of relevant evidence, their reasoning, and their imagination to develop a hypothesis. Sometimes scientists have more than one possible explanation for the same set of observations and evidence. Often when additional observations and testing are completed, scientists modify current scientific knowledge.

To test out hypotheses, scientists design experiments that will enable them to control conditions so that their results will be reliable. Scientists always repeat their experiment, doing it the same way it was done before and expecting to get very similar although not exact results. It is important to control conditions in order to make comparisons. Scientists sometimes are not sure what will happen because they don't know everything that might be having an effect on their experiment.

Create Meaning From the Experiment

Scientists analyze the data that are collected from the experiment to add to the existing body of scientific knowledge. They organize their data using data tables and graphs and then make inferences from the data to draw conclusions about whether their question was answered and the effectiveness of their experiments. Scientists also create meaning by comparing what they found to existing knowledge. The analysis of experiment data and process often leads to identification of related questions and future experiments.

Tell Others What Was Found

In the investigation process, scientists often work as a team, sharing findings with each other so that they may benefit from the results. Initially individual team members complete their own work and draw their own conclusions.

One way to introduce the wheel to students is to provide them with the graphic model and ask them to tell one reason why each section of the wheel is important to scientific investigation. The end of this appendix (pp. 86–88) includes several handouts that can be used with students to teach The Wheel of Scientific Investigation and Reasoning.

Concept Mapping

Overview

A concept map is a graphic representation of one's knowledge on a particular topic. Concept maps support learning, teaching, and evaluation (Novak & Gowin, 1984). Students clarify and extend their own thinking about a topic. Teachers find concept mapping useful for envisioning the scope of a lesson or unit. They also use student-developed concept maps as a way of measuring their progress. Meaningful concept maps often begin with a particular question (focus question) about a topic, event, or object.

Concept maps were developed in 1972 as part of research conducted by Dr. Joseph Novak's research at Cornell University. Dr. Novak was working with young children's understanding of science concepts. Students were interviewed by researchers who recorded their responses. The researchers sought an effective way to identify changes in students' understanding over time. Analysis of transcripts of students' verbal responses proved to be very difficult. Basing their work on Ausubel's cognitive psychology, Novak and his research colleagues began to represent the students' conceptual understanding in concept maps. Ausubel's cognitive psychology supports the idea that learning takes place through the assimilation of new concepts and propositions into existing concept and propositional frameworks.

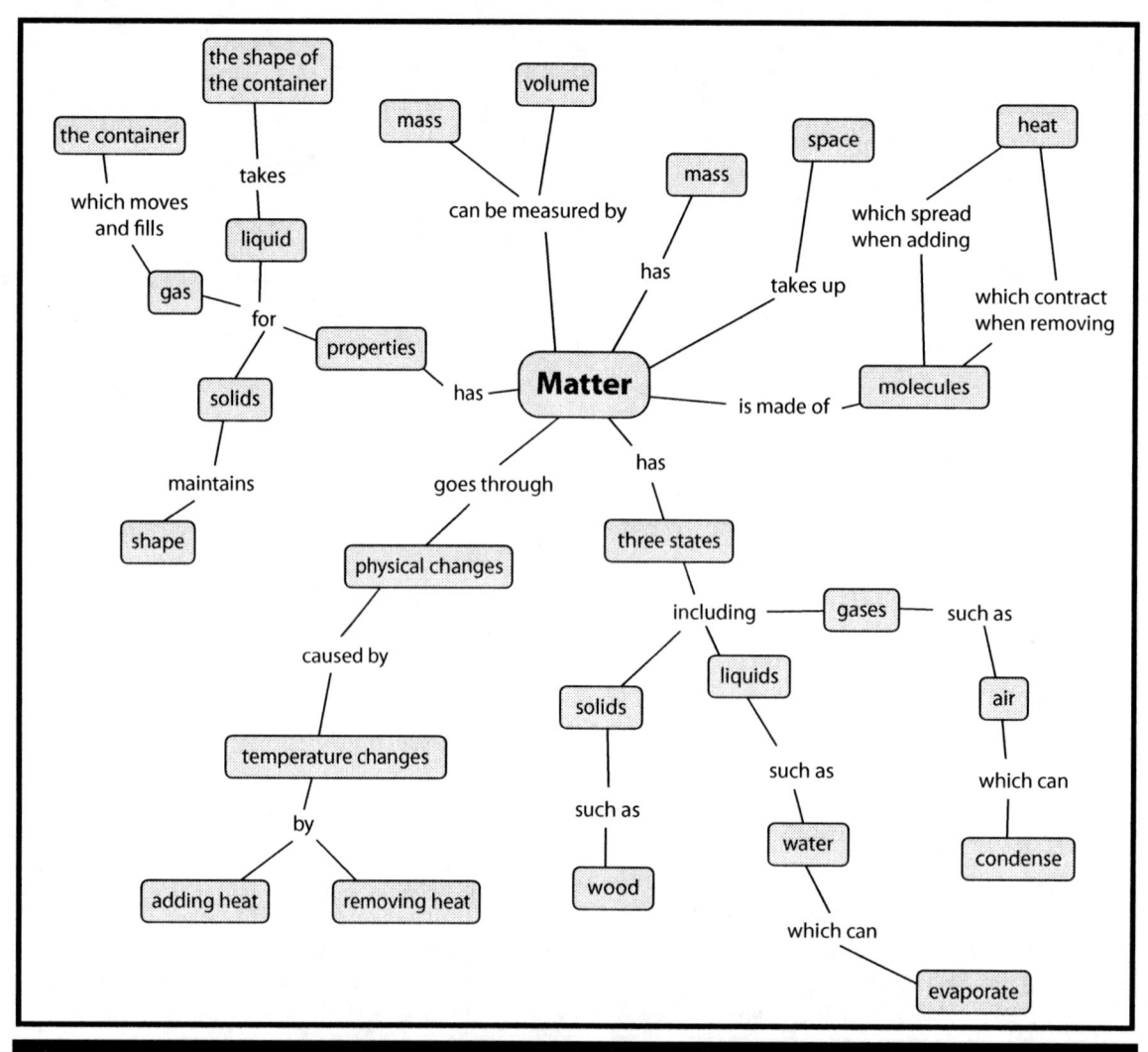

Figure 2. A concept map showing a student's understanding of matter.

As seen in Figure 2, concept maps show concepts and relationships between them. The concepts are contained within boxes or oval shapes and the connections between concepts are represented by lines with linking words.

Concepts are the students' perceived ideas generalized from particular experiences. Sometimes the concepts placed on the map may contain more than one word. Words placed on the line are linking words or phrases and the labels for the words that contain propositions. The propositions contain two or more concepts connected by linking words or phrases to form a meaningful statement.

The youngest students may view and develop concept maps making basic connections. They may begin with two concepts joined by a linking word. These "sentences" (propositions) become the building blocks for concept maps. Older students may begin to make multiple connections immediately as they develop their maps.

As students map their knowledge base, they begin to represent their conceptual understanding in a hierarchical manner. The broadest, most inclusive concepts are often found at the top of a concept map. More specific concepts and examples then follow.

Each Project Clarion unit contains an overview concept map, showing the essential knowledge included in the lessons and the connections students should be able to make as a result of their experiences within the unit. This overview may be useful as a classroom poster that the teacher and students may refer to throughout the unit.

Strategies to Prepare for Concept Mapping

The following strategies (adapted from Novak & Gowin, 1984) will help you prepare your students for the concept mapping activities.

What Do Words Mean?
1. Ask students to picture in their minds some common words (water, tree, door, box, pencil, dog). Start with "object" words, saying them one at a time, allowing time for students to picture each of them.
2. Create a class list of object words, asking students to name other objects they can picture in their minds to add to the list.
3. Next create a list of "event" words such as jumping, running, or eating. Ask students to envision each of these in their minds and encourage them to contribute to the class list of event words.
4. Give students a few words that are likely to be unfamiliar to most of them, asking if they can see a picture in their mind. Words should be short, such as data, cell, prey, or inertia. You might include a few simple words in another language. Ask students if they have any mind pictures.
5. Discuss the fact that words are useful to us because they convey meaning. This only happens when they can form a picture in their mind that represents the meaning they connect with the word.

What Is a Concept?
1. Introduce the word *concept* and explain that concept is the word we use to mean some kind of object or event we can picture in our mind. Refer back to the word lists previously developed as you discuss the word and ask if these are concepts. Can they see a picture in their mind for each of them? Let students know that when they come upon a word they do not know well enough to form a picture, they will just need to learn the concept associated with that new word. Learning new concepts is exciting and they will learn new ones in their science unit.
2. Provide each table with a few picture cards and ask students to take turns at their table naming some of the concepts included in the card.

What Are Linking Words?
1. Prepare a list of words such as the, is, are, when, that, then. Ask students if they can see a picture in their mind for each of these words. Explain that these are not concept words. These are linking words we use when we speak or write to link concept words together into sentences that have special meaning. Ask students if they have any words to add to the list. Label the list *Linking Words*.
2. Hold up two picture cards (sky and blue) and give students a sample sentence ("The sky is blue.") Ask students to tell you the concept words and the linking words in your sentence. Give another example.
3. Give each pair of students a few picture cards. Ask the students to work with partners to pick up two cards and then develop a sentence that links the two cards. They should take turns, with one partner making the sentence and the other identifying the concepts and the linking words. Ask them to repeat this a few times and then have several partners share their sentences.
4. Explain to students that it is easy to make up sentences and to read sentences where the printed labels (words) are familiar to them. Explain that reading and writing sentences is like making a link between two things (concepts) they already know. Practice this idea during reading time, asking students to find a sentence and analyze it for concepts and linking words.

Learning to Build a Concept Map (Novak & Gowin, 1984)

1. Make a list of 12–15 related and familiar concept words. Do not use words from the unit. Organize words from more general, more inclusive concepts to less general, more specific concepts. Here are two sets that work well.
   - city, buildings, streets, people, transportation, noise, elevator, stores, offices, one way, taxis, limousines, subway, workers, tourists. This set can be used in conjunction with the children' book, *Do Skyscrapers Touch the Sky?: First Questions and Answers About the City* by TIME-Life.
   - farm, animals, farmer, cow, horse, crops, soil, corn, potatoes, barn, machinery, tractor, harvest, food

2. Tell students that they are going to participate in an activity that uses their understanding of concepts and linking words. Tell them that they will develop a concept map. First, show a simple concept map (my pet, a school bus) on chart paper or with an electronic device (computer, smart board, overhead projector). Give students one example of a "sentence" contained in the map. Ask them to tell the concept words and the linking words. Then ask students to find another sentence and describe the parts. Ask students if they can think of other links to add to the map. Give partners a copy of the map and ask them to add one or more links to the map.
3. Give partners a list of related words and ask them to play around with them until they have selected two or more to link together. Ask students to paste their words on their papers and write in the linking words.
4. Ask student to make a concept map, using a few words you provide, based on a familiar topic. Allow students to add other words and pictures as they wish. Ask students to share their maps with partners and then share a few with the whole class.

Concept Mapping Practice Activities

1. Provide students with picture cards and ask them to select two things that go together in some way. Students should tell what they selected and then make a sentence about the two objects that show a link.
2. Give partners a set of related picture cards and a topic. Also provide the partners with a piece of yarn. Ask students to work together to decide on a linking sentence. When they have a good link, they should hold up their cards and link themselves together stretching the yarn in their hands.
3. Give students a copy of a very basic concept map with some blank areas. Provide the appropriate responses on paper for students to cut out and add to the map to make it complete.
4. Provide a center activity with a list of linking words and picture cards. Use either general pictures or pictures specific to the unit. Encourage students to practice making mapping sentences by using two cards and connecting them with linking words.
5. Ask students to create their own pictures that show the linking of two concepts.
6. Ask students to select three concept pictures and link them together.
7. Ask students to create pictures that show the linking of three concepts they have selected from the set of concept cards.
8. Given a set of related words, ask student to develop a concept map on the table, using the cards and then adding linking words on small blank cards.

9. Given a set of related words, ask students to develop a concept map on paper, either gluing the cards onto a large sheet or drawing the objects and adding the linking words.
10. Ask students a question about a particular topic and ask them to use a bank of words and or pictures to create a concept map that responds to the question. Encourage students to add words to the bank to use in the map.

Using Concept Mapping in Unit Lessons

Rationale: Practice in using concept maps supports student learning as they begin to build upon known concepts. Students begin to add new concepts to their initial understanding of a topic and to make new connections between concepts. The use of concept maps within the lessons also helps teachers to recognize students' conceptual frameworks so that instruction can be adapted as necessary. Student-developed maps also frequently reveal student misconceptions in science.

Strategies:
1. Provide a large unit concept map as a constant poster on the wall, referring to it at critical times to reinforce new learning.
2. Use some aspect of concept mapping as a warm-up or review of the lesson. You can display a concept map of what is going to be experienced in the lesson or as a review at the end of the lesson.
3. Use concept mapping "sentences" to reinforce new concepts in the lesson, providing students with opportunities to make links with their new knowledge.
4. Encourage students to take home several of the key concept words or pictures for sharing with parents or guardians. Ask students to show their families how they can link two of the concepts.
5. Develop a large concept map for the overarching concept in your unit, referring to the generalizations and asking students to make links to add to the map with sticky notes.

The Frayer Model of Vocabulary Development

The Frayer Model of Vocabulary Development (Frayer, Frederick, & Klausmeier, 1969) provides students with a graphic organizer that asks them to think about and describe the meaning of a word or concept (see Figures 3 and 4 for examples of blank and completed Frayer Model organizers). This process enables them to strengthen their understanding of vocabulary words. Through the model students are required to consider the important characteristics of the word and to provide examples and nonexamples of the concept. This model has similarities to the Taba Concept Development Model.

In introducing the Frayer Model to your students, demonstrate its use on large chart paper. Begin with a word all students know such as rock, umbrella, or shoe, placing it on the graphic model. First, ask the students to define the word in their own words. Record a definition that represents their common knowledge. Next, ask students to give specific characteristics of the word/concept or facts they know about it. Record these ideas. Then ask students to offer examples of the idea and then nonexamples to finish the graphic.

Another way to use the Frayer Model is to provide students with examples and nonexamples and ask them to consider what word or concept is being analyzed. You can provide similar exercises by filling in some portions of the graphic and asking students to complete the remaining sections.

Definition	Characteristics (What a Scientist Does)
"...a person who studies nature and the physical world by testing, experimenting, and measuring"	• •
Examples	Nonexamples
• •	• •

Scientist (center)

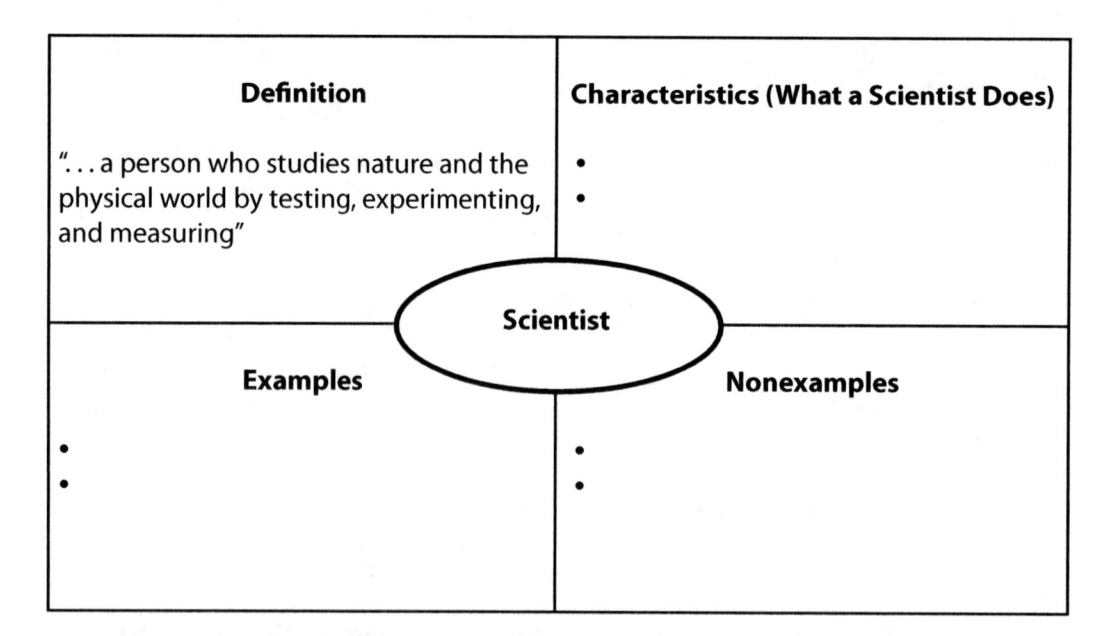

Figure 3. Blank Frayer Model of Vocabulary Development graphic.

Definition	Characteristics (What a Scientist Does)
"...a person who studies nature and the physical world by testing, experimenting, and measuring"	• Ask questions. • Make observations. • Make predictions and/or hypotheses. • Collects, classify, and analyze data. • Design experiments. • Draw inferences. • Communicate findings.
Examples	Nonexamples
• Astronomers—study the universe (planets, stars, etc.) • Biologists—study life (plants and animals) • Geologists—study the earth's layers of soil and rocks. • Physicists—study matter and energy	• An entertainer • A poet • A banker

Scientist (center)

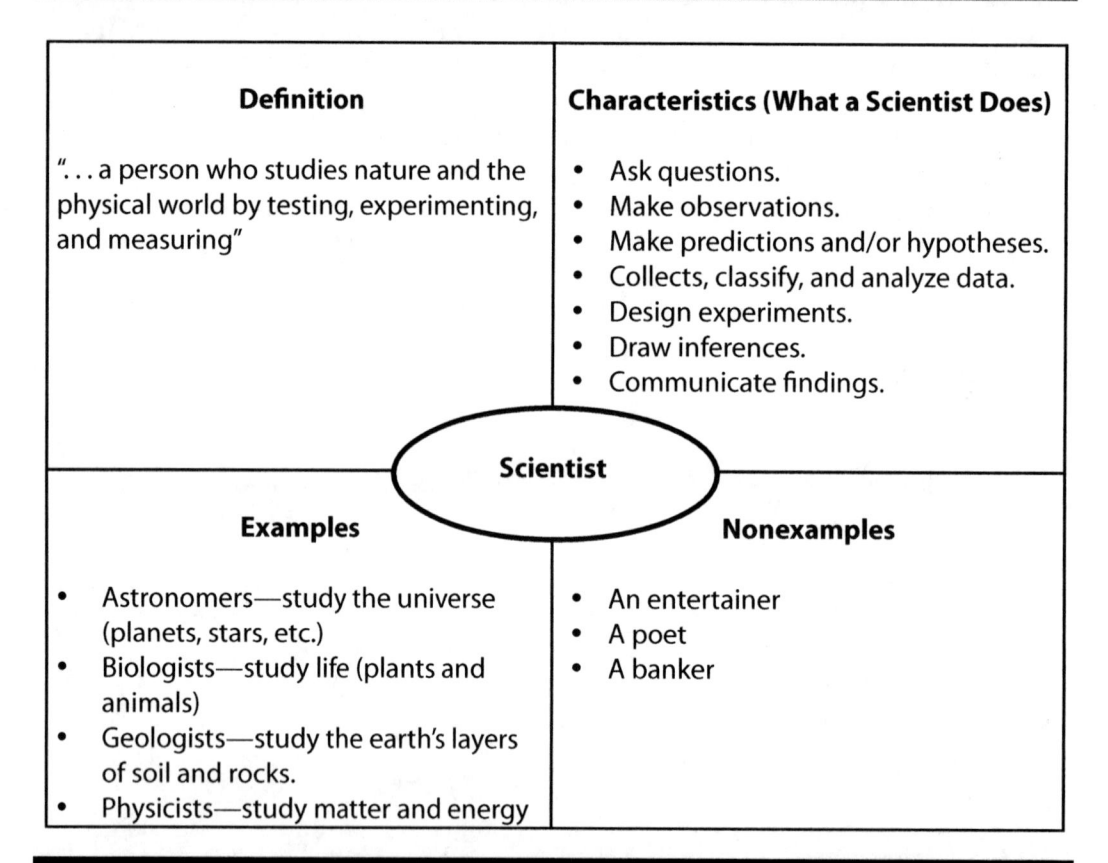

Figure 4. Completed graphic organizer for Frayer Model.

As students share ideas, note the level of understanding of the group and of individual students. As the unit is taught, certain vocabulary words may need this type of expanded thinking to support student readiness for using the vocabulary in the science activities. You may want students to maintain individual notebooks of words so that they can refer back to them in their work.

Name:_____ Date:_____

The Wheel of Scientific Investigation and Reasoning

Make Observations
- Use your curiosity.
- Find something of interest to study.
- Use your senses to learn.

Ask Questions
- Identify all of the questions you have.
- Select ONE question you want to answer.

Learn More
- Find what you need to know.
- Find what others know.
- Learn more through observations.
- Reexamine your question.

Design and Conduct the Experiment
- Form a hypothesis from your question.
- List experiment steps.
- Identify materials you need.
- Conduct experiment.
- Record data.

Create Meaning
- Organize your data.
- Analyze data.
- Make inferences and draw conclusions.
- Check to see if you answered your question.
- Think of related questions.

Tell Others What Was Found
- Select an audience.
- Decide on the best way to communicate.
- Include data tables.
- Report conclusions.

Scientific Investigation and Reasoning

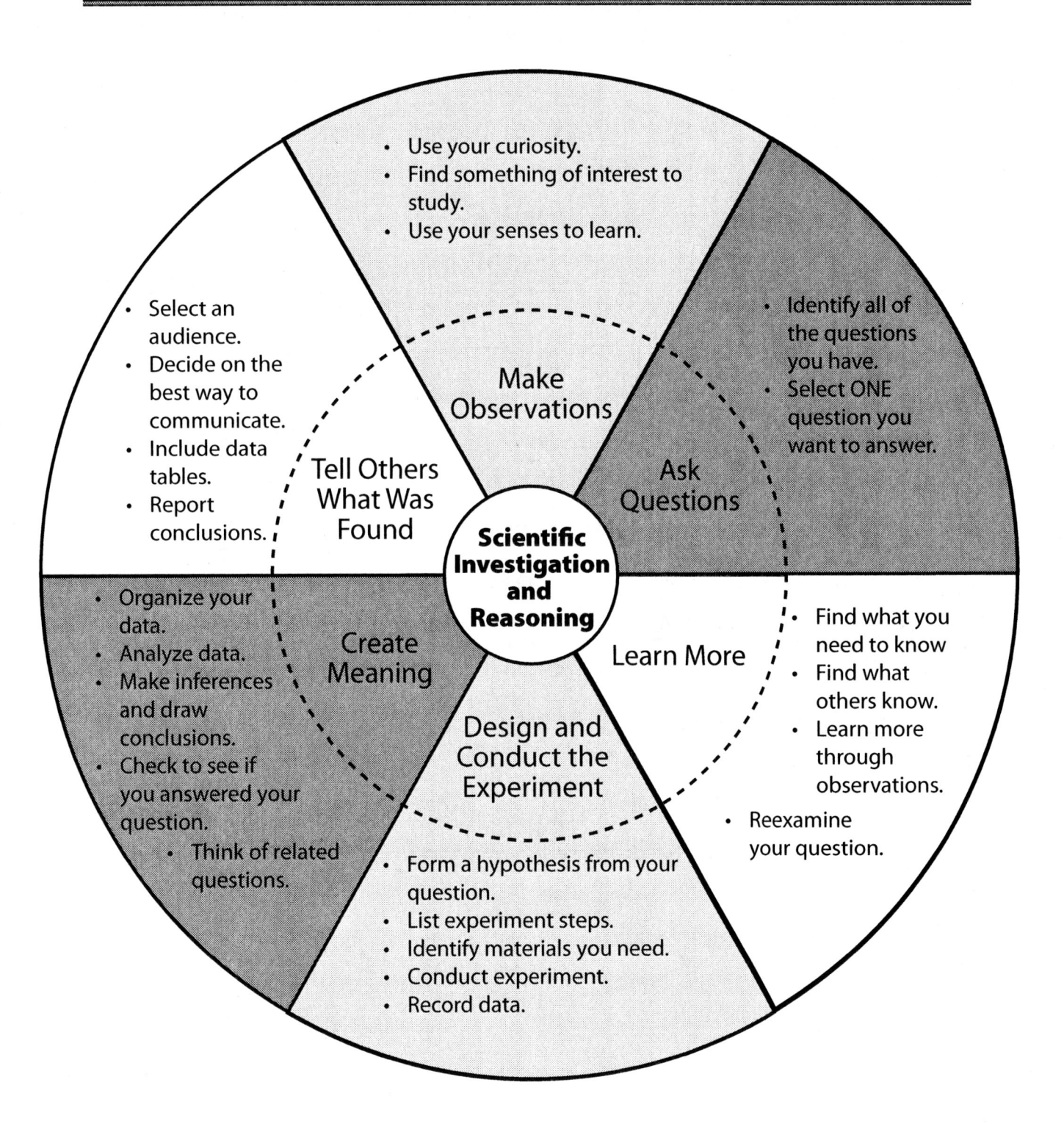

© Prufrock Press Inc. • *Water Works*
This page may be photocopied or reproduced with permission for classroom use only.

Name:_____ Date:_____

What Scientists Do...
The Wheel of Scientific Investigation and Reasoning

- Make Observations
- Ask Questions
- Learn More
- Design and Conduct the Experiment
- Create Meaning
- Tell Others What Was Found

Scientific Investigation and Reasoning

Name:_____ Date:_____

Planning Wheel of Scientific Investigation and Reasoning

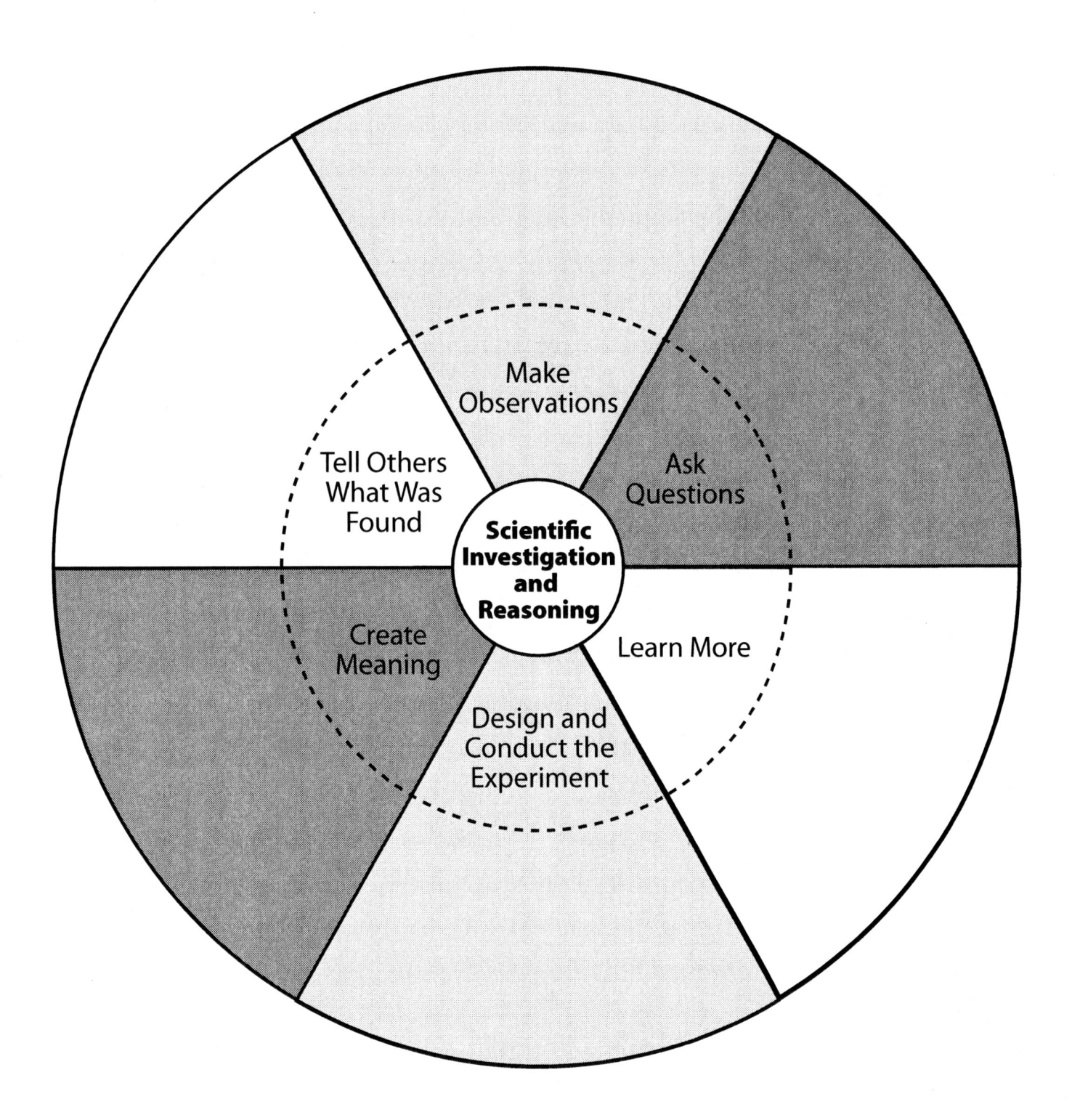

- Make Observations
- Ask Questions
- Learn More
- Design and Conduct the Experiment
- Create Meaning
- Tell Others What Was Found

Scientific Investigation and Reasoning

Appendix C: Basic Concepts

Basic Concept Development

Often preschoolers' and primary grade students' understanding of science concepts and skills is inhibited by lack of understanding of basic concepts related to describing nature and elements of science (e.g., colors, shapes, sizes, textures). Therefore, it is important for teachers to determine which basic concepts students have not mastered. Teachers should take every opportunity to incorporate as many concepts as possible into every unit lesson.

Basic Concept Development Program

One basic concept development program is the Bracken Basic Concepts program developed by Bruce Bracken. The Bracken Basic Concept Scale-Revised (Bracken, 1998) identifies 308 basic language concepts that are foundational and important to students' cognitive development and acquisition of academic content knowledge. These concepts are grouped conceptually into the following 11 categories:
- colors,
- letter identification,
- numbers/counting,
- sizes,
- comparisons,
- shapes,
- direction/position,
- self- and social awareness,
- texture/material,
- quantity, and
- time/sequence.

Bracken Basic Concepts were originally used in the field tests for the Project Clarion science units.

Appendix D: Assessment Package

Preassessment Directions to the Teacher

Instructional Purpose: To determine prior knowledge of unit content.

Instructional Time:
- Concept assessment: 30 minutes, including preteaching activity
- Scientific process assessment: 20 minutes
- Content assessment: 30 minutes, including preteaching activity

Materials/Resources/Equipment Needed:
- Copies of preassessments and preteaching materials for unit concept, process, and content (pp. 91–113)
- Pencils

Activities:
1. Explain to students that the class is beginning a new unit of study. Tell them that they will be completing a preassessment to determine what they already know about the topic. Assure them that the assessment is not for a grade and encourage them to do their best.
2. Collect the preassessments and debrief with students to begin building their understanding of the unit concept, process, and content. Briefly review each assessment and discuss some of the responses in general, indicating that this unit will provide them with more knowledge and skills than they now have.
3. Score the preassessments, using the rubrics provided. Keep the scores for diagnostic purposes in organizing grouping and various activities during the unit.

Name:_____ Date:_____

Preteaching for Change
Concept Assessment

Some changes can be caused by people. Look at the following examples and think of a way to *change* them:

1. If I wanted to change a bicycle, I could

2. If I wanted to change my clothes, I would

3. If I wanted to change the color of a house, I could

Name:_____ Date:_____

Other changes occur naturally. Look at the following changes from the natural world.

4. A seed changes into a

5. A baby changes into a

6. An ice cube can change into

Name:_____ Date:_____

Draw a picture of something that changes. Then, draw a picture of what it changes into.

Name:_____ Date:_____

Preassessment for Change Concept

What is change? In each box draw a picture or write a word for something that changes.

© Prufrock Press Inc. • *Water Works*
This page may be photocopied or reproduced with permission for classroom use only.

Name:_____ Date:_____

Draw a picture of something in your life that changes and show how it changes. Include as many details as you can.

Name:_____ Date:_____

Draw five ways a tree could change or be changed.

Name:_____ Date:_____

Name:_____ Date:_____

Scoring Rubric for Change Concept

		5	4	3	2	1	0
1	**Examples of the Concept**	At least 9–10 appropriate examples are given.	7–8 appropriate examples are given.	5–6 appropriate examples are given.	3–4 appropriate examples are given.	1–2 appropriate examples are given.	No examples are given.
2	**Drawing of Before-After**	The drawing contains five well-defined pictures depicting a before-after situation.	The drawing contains four elements of before-after situations.	The drawing contains three picture elements that depict a before-after situation.	The drawing contains two elements of before-after relationships.	The drawing contains only one element of a before-after relationship.	The drawing contains no elements of a before-after relationship.
3	**Types of Change**	Five different types of changes are identified.	Four different types of changes are identified.	Three different types of changes are identified.	Two different types of changes are identified.	One different type of change is identified.	No type of change is identified.

Total points: ____ /15

Preteaching for Scientific Process Assessment

Materials Needed:
- Clear container
- Spoon
- Salt
- Warm water

Activities:
1. Prepare students for the unit preassessment by providing an activity that models an experiment to answer the question, "Does salt dissolve in water?"
2. Tell students that you are going to do an experiment to answer the question, "Does salt dissolve in water?" Ask them to make a prediction. Do they think salt dissolves in water?
3. Conduct the experiment. Ask students what they will need to determine whether or not their prediction is correct. What materials will they need? Elicit responses for materials and list on chart paper. Show each material as it is mentioned.
4. Now tell students that they will perform the experiment. Ask a student to help you pour the salt into the water and another student to stir it. Tell students to observe what happens.
    a. Did the salt dissolve? Was their prediction correct?
    b. What do we mean by dissolve? (Dissolve means to "seem to disappear when mixed with liquid" [Scholastic, 1996].)
5. Tell students they are going to try the experiment again to see if they get the same results. Follow the same steps as above, recording the results on a simple chart and asking the students to mark yes or no for each trial's question of "Did the salt dissolve in water?"
6. Review with students the fact that we got the same answer each time. That means that we will probably get the same response again. Salt does dissolve in water.
7. Say to students, "Today we learned that some things like salt dissolve in water."

Preassessment for Scientific Process

1. Assess students in groups of 4–6.
2. Tell students they are going to think like scientists. Say to students, "I have a scientific question for you: Does sand dissolve in water? You are going to think about whether or not sand dissolves in water. We will work together to look at some pictures and select an answer to some questions about an experiment to find out if sand dissolves in water."
3. Pass out the packet of assessment record sheets (see pp. 101–105). Ask students to look at the first sheet: Preassessment: Does Sand Dissolve in Water? Ask them to write their name on the paper. Direct them to think about the two pictures and make a prediction about whether or not sand dissolves in water. Tell students to put an X in the box under the picture that shows their prediction—sand does not dissolve in water or sand does dissolve in water. Picture choices are:
    a. Clear container with water and sand on the bottom.
    b. Clear container with water and no sand on the bottom.

4. Next ask students to think about what materials they will need for their experiment. Look at the What Materials Will You Need? handout. Ask students to put an X under each picture that shows a material that will be used in the experiment. Picture choices are:
    a. Clear container
    b. Spoon
    c. Sand
    d. Salt
    e. Water
    f. Milk

5. Present each student with a set of four cards showing pictures of the steps in the experiment (p. 103). Tell the students to select the pictures that show the steps they would take for the experiment. Picture choices are (1) gathering the materials, (2) pouring in water, (3) pouring in sand, (4) stirring the mixture. Students will use all of the pictures.
6. Instruct students to put the steps they selected in the correct order—which comes first, second, and so forth. Check to see each student's response and record.
7. Ask students to look at the table on p. 103 and decide whether the table shows that sand dissolves in water or salt does not dissolve in water. Students should put an X in the correct box.
8. Ask students to look at the What Will Dissolve? handout. The materials are: salt, oatmeal, crayon, JELL-O, rock, twig, leaf, and sugar. Direct students to think about things that probably dissolve in water and to place an X in each box under a picture that shows something that will dissolve. Which of these materials will dissolve?

Name: _____ Date: _____

Preassessment: Does Sand Dissolve in Water?

Does sand dissolve in water? Put an X in the box that matches your prediction.

☐   ☐

Name:_____ Date:_____

What Materials Will You Need?

What materials do you need to conduct your experiment? Put an X in the box of each material you would use.

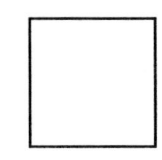

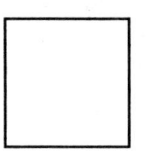

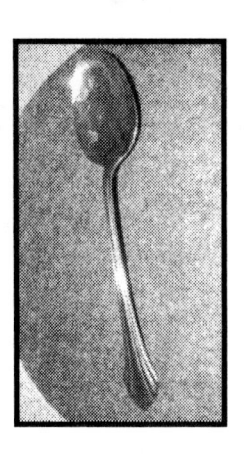

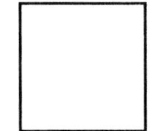

Name:_____ Date:_____

How Would You Conduct Your Experiment?

Cut out the pictures below and place them in order of the steps of the water and sand experiment.

© Prufrock Press Inc. • *Water Works*
This page may be photocopied or reproduced with permission for classroom use only.

Name:_____ Date:_____

What Does This Table Show?

Did the sand dissolve in water?

Cassidy	No
Lowell	No
Sandy	No
Adrian	No
Leslie	No
Lincoln	No
Jonah	No
Chwee	No
Sun	No

___ Yes, the sand dissolved in water.

___ No, the sand did not dissolve in water.

© Prufrock Press Inc. • *Water Works*
This page may be photocopied or reproduced with permission for classroom use only.

104

Name:_____ Date:_____

What Will Dissolve?

Put an X in the box below each picture that shows something that will dissolve in water.

© Prufrock Press Inc. • *Water Works*
This page may be photocopied or reproduced with permission for classroom use only.

Project Clarion Scoring Guide: Scientific Process Performance-Based Assessment

Student _____ Teacher _____
Grade Level _____
School _____ Date _____

Criteria

Selects a prediction: Does sand dissolve in water? (p. 101; up to 1 point)
Scoring guide: Score the two glasses of water/sand as being either correct or incorrect (i.e., 1 pt or 0 pt credit). Give 1 point if student selects the glass with sand at the bottom.

Selects materials needed. (p. 102; up to 6 points)
Scoring guide: A total of up to 6 points is earned for checking the sand, empty glass, spoon, and water and not checking salt or milk.

Sequences steps. (p. 103; up to 4 points)
Scoring guide: One point is earned for each picture in its appropriate order. A total of up to 4 points may be given. The following order is correct: (1) the girl sitting with the ingredients in front of her, (2) the girl pouring water, (3) the girl pouring in sand, and (4) the girl mixing.

Selects the appropriate interpretation of the data table provided. (p. 104; up to 2 points)
Scoring guide: Two points awarded for the "No" response.

Selects a prediction: What will dissolve? (p. 105; up to 9 points)
Scoring guide: One point should be given for each of the boxes being checked or not checked accurately. Checks should appear for salt, JELL-O, and sugar. No checks should appear for the remaining items. (3 points if each is noted.)

Total possible points: ____ /22

Preteaching for Content Preassessment

Explain to students that sometimes we know a lot about something even before our teachers teach it in school. Sometimes we don't know very much at all, but we like to learn new things.

For example, ask students, "What would you think about if someone asked you to tell all you know about how *farms* work? What are some of the words you would use?" List these on a chart. Then ask, "What are some of the things that happen on a farm?" List these on your chart as well. Then say, "I am going to show you a way I might tell about everything I know about how farms work." Begin a concept map on a large sheet of paper, using pictures and words, making simple links and emphasizing these links. Ask students to make their own maps on their drawing paper. This practice activity can be done with a partner. Share some of the resulting concept maps, encouraging students to articulate their links.

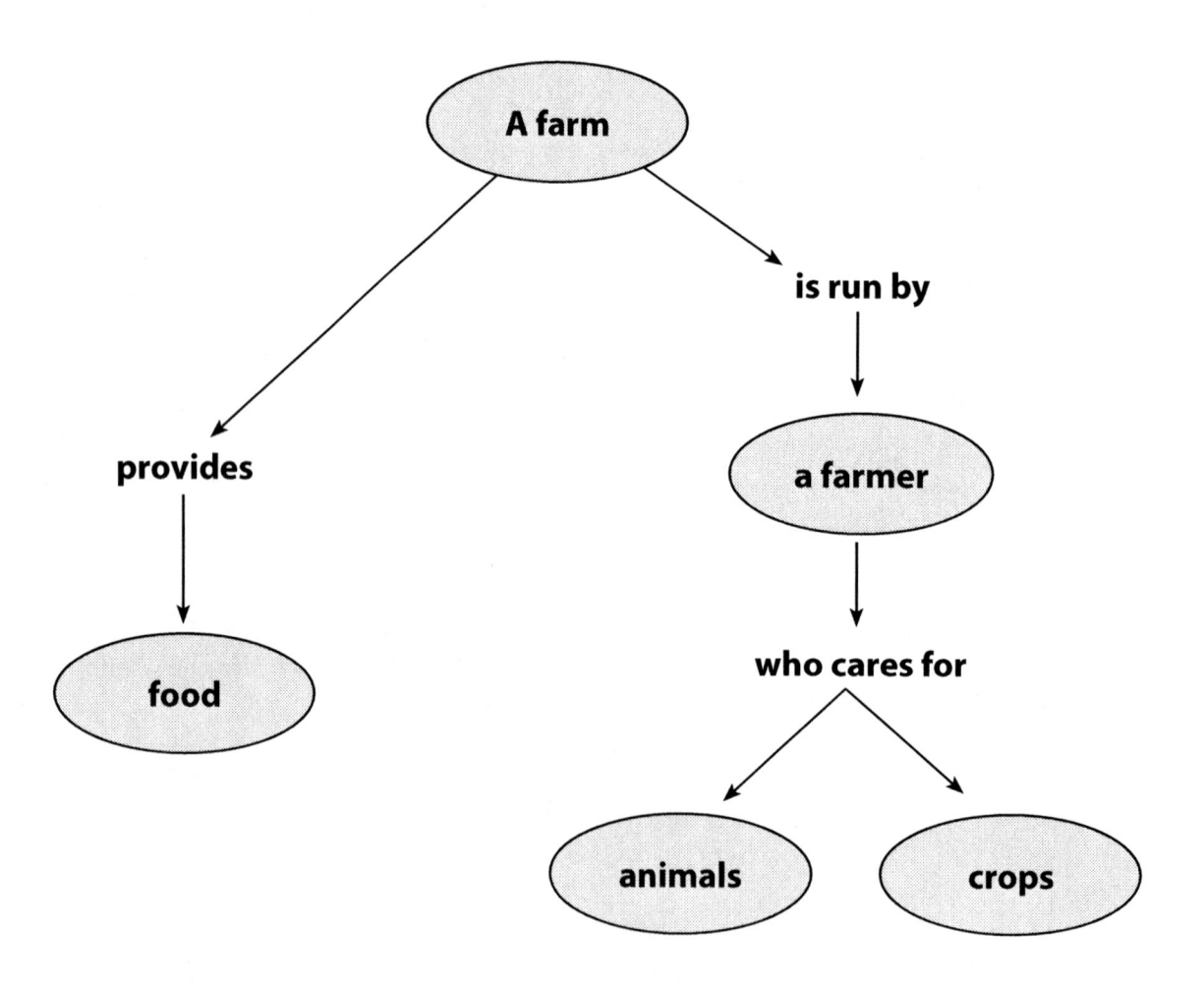

```
                    ┌─────────┐
                    │ A farm  │
                    └─────────┘
                   ╱           ╲
            provides         is run by
                 ↓               ↓
            ┌────────┐      ┌─────────┐
            │  food  │      │ a farmer│
            └────────┘      └─────────┘
                                 ↓
                            who cares for
                             ╱        ╲
                            ↓          ↓
                      ┌────────┐  ┌────────┐
                      │animals │  │ crops  │
                      └────────┘  └────────┘
```

Preassessment for Content
Water Works

Start with these opening statements to your class: "Today I would like you to think about all the things you know about water. Think about the connections you can make. You will be completing a concept map, just like the ones you did when we discussed the farm. Look at the word bank and the concept map. You will use some of the word bank words to fill in the parts of the concept map. Some words are just extras that you won't need. Remember, a concept map is used to tell about what we know and make connections."

Kindergarten

Direct students to use the word bank to complete the assessment. Students also may use other responses that they come up with on their own. Tell students to draw a picture or write the word or letter for their responses in the appropriate blanks. Each correct response earns one point. Students may enter the word *or* just the letter corresponding to the word *or* come up with their own word.

First Grade

Direct students to complete the assessment with appropriate words, pictures, or their own choices of words. Each correct response earns one point.

Name: _____ Date: _____

Water Works Preassessment Concept Map

Fill in the map provided with as much as you know about water.

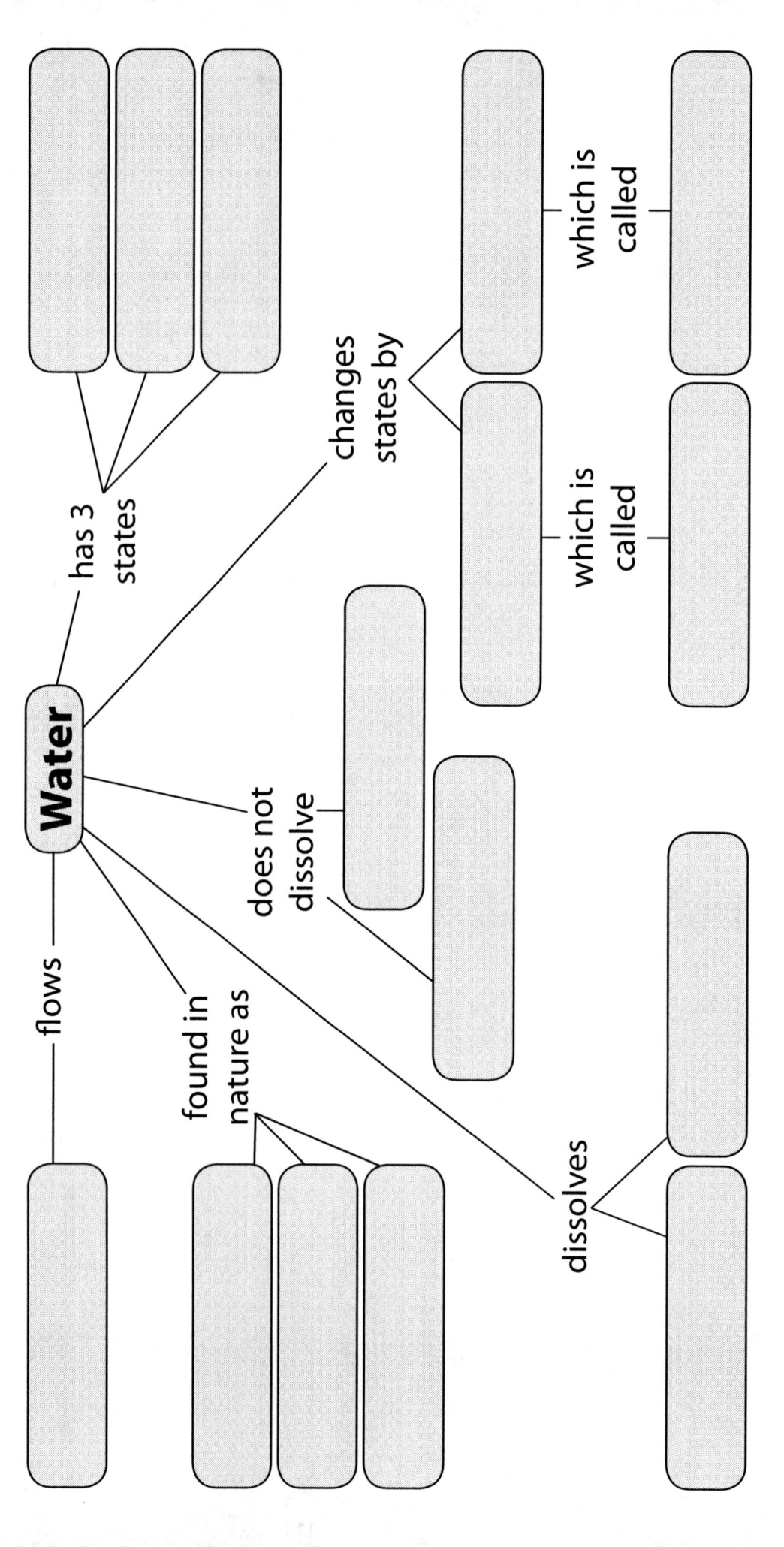

Water
- has 3 states → [ ] [ ] [ ]
- changes states by → [ ] — which is called → [ ]
- changes states by → [ ] — which is called → [ ]
- does not dissolve → [ ]
- dissolves → [ ] [ ]
- found in nature as → [ ] [ ] [ ]
- flows → [ ]

© Prufrock Press Inc. • Water Works
This page may be photocopied or reproduced with permission for classroom use only.

Name: _____ Date: _____

Concept Map Word Bank

flows	up	everywhere	even	downhill	over	everywhere
found in nature as	ocean	mountain	river	valley	desert	lake
has 3 states	floating	solid	circular	uneven	liquid	gas
changes states by	cooling	mixing	heating	burning	testing	stirring
which is called	condensation	creation	permutation	vacation	evaporation	violation
dissolves	oil	sugar	cone	salt	wood	metal
does not dissolve	sugar	wood	oil	cone	salt	rock

110

© Prufrock Press Inc. • *Water Works*
This page may be photocopied or reproduced with permission for classroom use only.

Name:_____ Date:_____

Water Works **Concept Preassessment**

I also know this about water:

1. _____

2. _____

3. _____

4. _____

5. _____

Project Clarion Scoring Guide: Content Assessment Performance-Based Assessment

Student _____ Teacher _____

Grade Level _____

School _____ Date _____

Criteria

Water Works **Preassessment Concept Map** (p. 109; up to 15 points)
Scoring guide: Score 1 point for each correct response in the concept map. Note that the student may have chosen a word that is not in the word bank. Score 1 point as long as the word(s) complete the link accurately. Students also may receive a point for each picture that accurately completes a link.

Water Works **Concept Preassessment: "I also know . . ."** (p. 111; up to 5 points)
Scoring guide: Score 1 point for each accurate and different response.

Total possible points: ____ /20

Name: _____ Date: _____

Sample Concept Map for Water Works

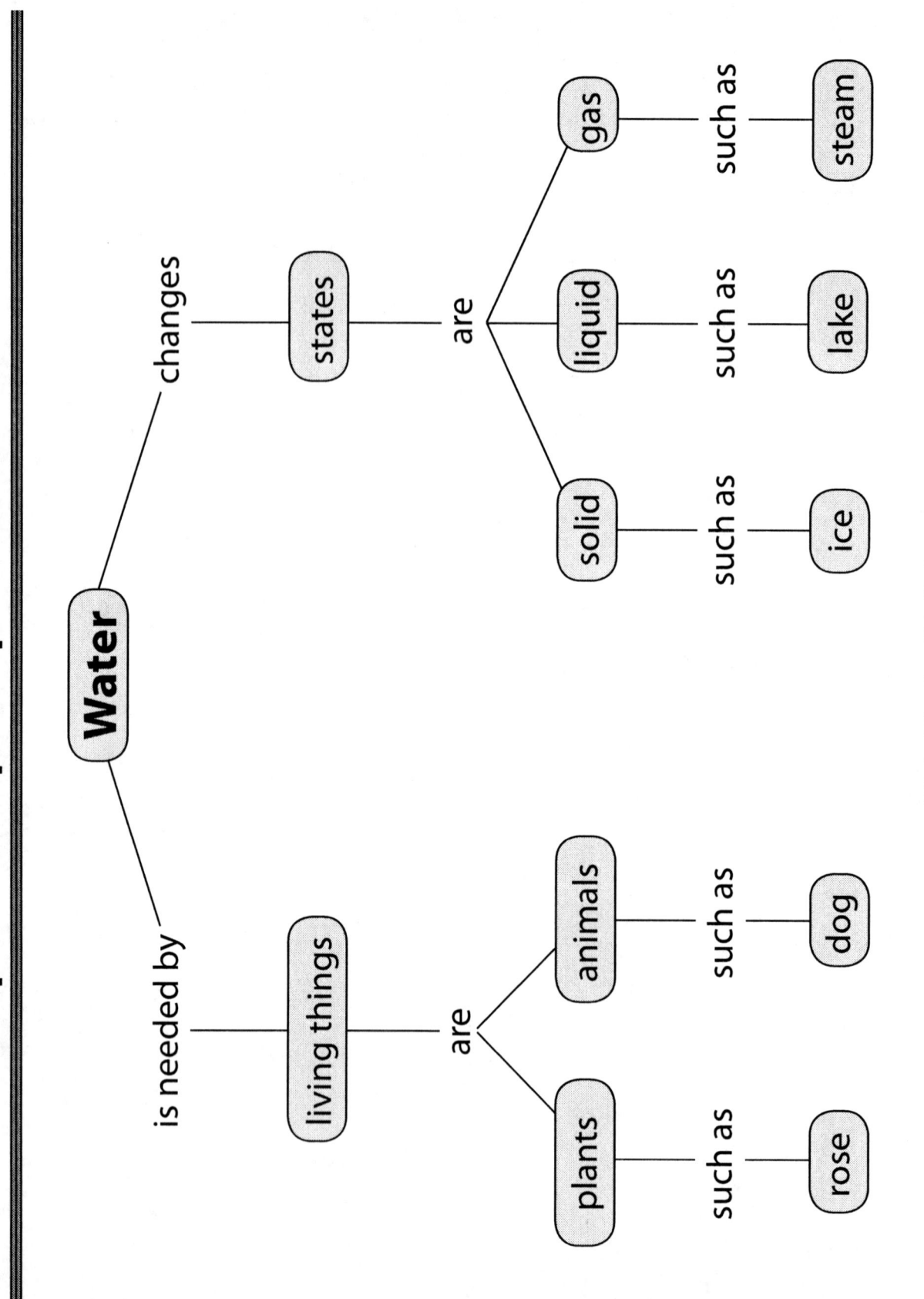

- **Water**
  - is needed by → living things
    - are → animals
      - such as → dog
    - are → plants
      - such as → rose
  - changes → states
    - are → solid
      - such as → ice
    - are → liquid
      - such as → lake
    - are → gas
      - such as → steam

Postassessment Directions for the Teacher

Instructional Purpose: To assess student knowledge of unit content.

Instructional Time:
- Concept assessment: 30 minutes, including preteaching activity
- Scientific process assessment: 20 minutes
- Content assessment: 30 minutes, including preteaching activity

Materials/Resources/Equipment Needed:
- Copies of postassessments for unit concept, process, and content (pp. 115–128)
- Pencils

Activities: Give each student a copy of the postassessments to complete in the order noted above. The assessments should take no more than 80 minutes in all. Explain that the assessment will be used to see how much students have learned during the unit.

Scoring: Use rubrics contained in preassessment sections for concept, scientific process, and content.

Name: _____   Date: _____

Postassessment for Change Concept

What is change? In each box draw a picture or write a word for something that changes.

Name:_____ Date:_____

Draw a picture of something in your life that changes and show how it changes. Include as many details as you can.

Name:

Name:_____ Date:_____

Draw five ways a tree could change or be changed.

Name:_____ Date:_____

Postassessment for Scientific Process

1. Assess students in groups of 4–6.
2. Tell students they are going to think like scientists. Say to students, "I have a scientific question for you: Does sand dissolve in water? You are going to think about whether or not sand dissolves in water. We will work together to look at some pictures and select an answer to some questions about an experiment to find out if sand dissolves in water."
3. Pass out the packet of assessment record sheets (see pp. 120–124). Ask students to look at the first sheet: Preassessment: Does Sand Dissolve in Water? Ask them to write their name on the paper. Direct them to think about the two pictures and make a prediction about whether or not sand dissolves in water. Tell students to put an X in the box under the picture that shows their prediction—sand does not dissolve in water or sand does dissolve in water. Picture choices are:
    a. Clear container with water and sand on the bottom.
    b. Clear container with water and no sand on the bottom.

4. Next ask students to think about what materials they will need for their experiment. Look at the What Materials Will You Need? handout. Ask students to put an X under each picture that shows a material that will be used in the experiment. Picture choices are:
    a. Clear container
    b. Spoon
    c. Sand
    d. Salt
    e. Water
    f. Milk

5. Present each student with a set of four cards showing pictures of the steps in the experiment (p. 122). Tell the students to select the pictures that show the steps they would take for the experiment. Picture choices are (1) gathering the materials, (2) pouring in water, (3) pouring in sand, (4) stirring the mixture. Students will use all of the pictures.
6. Instruct students to put the steps they selected in the correct order—which comes first, second, and so forth. Check to see each student's response and record.
7. Ask students to look at the table on p. 123 and decide whether the table shows that sand dissolves in water or salt does not dissolve in water. Students should put an x in the correct box.
8. Ask students to look at the What Will Dissolve? handout. The materials are: salt, oatmeal, crayon, JELL-O, rock, twig, leaf, and sugar. Direct students to think about things that probably dissolve in water and to place an X in each box under a picture that shows something that will dissolve. Which of these materials will dissolve?

Name:_____ Date:_____

Postassessment:
Does Sand Dissolve in Water?

Does sand dissolve in water? Put an X in the box that matches your prediction.

☐   ☐

© Prufrock Press Inc. • *Water Works*
This page may be photocopied or reproduced with permission for classroom use only.

Name:_____ Date:_____

Postassessment:
What Materials Will You Need?

What materials do you need to conduct your experiment? Put an X in the box of each material you would use.

☐   ☐   ☐

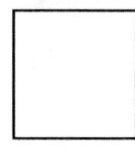

☐   ☐   ☐

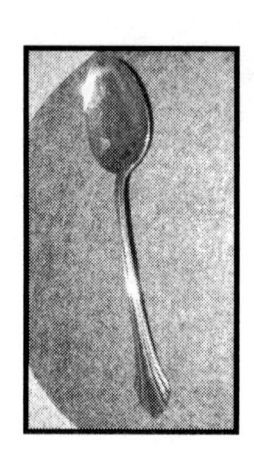

Name:_____ Date:_____

Postassessment: How Would You Conduct Your Experiment?

Cut out the pictures below and place them in order of the steps of the water and sand experiment.

© Prufrock Press Inc. • *Water Works*
This page may be photocopied or reproduced with permission for classroom use only.

Name:_____ Date:_____

Postassessment:
What Does This Table Show?

Did the sand dissolve in water?

Cassidy	No
Lowell	No
Sandy	No
Adrian	No
Leslie	No
Lincoln	No
Jonah	No
Chwee	No
Sun	No

___ Yes, the sand dissolved in water.

___ No, the sand did not dissolve in water.

Name:_____ Date:_____

Postassessment: What Will Dissolve?

Put an X in the box below each picture that shows something that will dissolve in water.

© Prufrock Press Inc. • *Water Works*
This page may be photocopied or reproduced with permission for classroom use only.

Postassessment for Content
Water Works

Start with these opening statements to your class: "Today I would like you to think about all the things you know about water. Think about the connections you can make. You will be completing a concept map, just like the ones you did when we discussed the farm. Look at the word bank and the concept map. You will use some of the word bank words to fill in the parts of the concept map. Some words are just extras that you won't need. Remember, a concept map is used to tell about what we know and make connections."

Kindergarten

Direct students to use the word bank to complete the assessment. Students also may use other responses that they come up with on their own. Tell students to draw a picture or write the word or letter for their responses in the appropriate blanks. Each correct response earns one point. Students may enter the word *or* just the letter corresponding to the word *or* come up with their own word.

First Grade

Direct students to complete the assessment with appropriate words, pictures, or their own choices of words. Each correct response earns one point.

Name: _____ Date: _____

Water Works Postassessment Concept Map

Fill in the map provided with as much as you know about water.

Name: _____ Date: _____

Concept Map Word Bank

flows	up	everywhere	even	downhill	over	everywhere
found in nature as	ocean	mountain	river	valley	desert	lake
has 3 states	floating	solid	circular	uneven	liquid	gas
changes states by	cooling	mixing	heating	burning	testing	stirring
which is called	condensation	creation	permutation	vacation	evaporation	violation
dissolves	oil	sugar	cone	salt	wood	metal
does not dissolve	sugar	wood	oil	cone	salt	rock

127

Name:_____ Date:_____

Water Works Concept Postassessment

I also know this about water:

1. _____

2. _____

3. _____

4. _____

5. _____

References

Bracken, B. (1998). *Bracken Basic Concept Scale–Revised*. San Antonio, TX: Harcourt Assessments.

Frayer, D. A., Frederick, W. C., & Klausmeier, H. J. (1969). *A schema for testing the level of concept mastery* (Technical Report No. 16). Madison: The University of Wisconsin, Wisconsin Research and Development Center for Cognitive Learning.

Novak, J., & Gowin, B. D. (1984). *Learning how to learn*. New York: Cambridge University Press.

Scholastic. (Eds.). (1996). *Scholastic children's dictionary* (Rev. ed.). New York: Author.

Taba, H. (1962). *Curriculum development, theory and practice*. New York: Harcourt Brace.